ADVENTURES IN THE
AFTERLIFE

WILLIAM BUHLMAN

Osprey Press
Millsboro, Delaware

ISBN: 1453786058
ISBN-13: 978-1453786055

Library of Congress Control Number: 2010912870
CreateSpace Independent Publishing Platform
North Charleston, South Carolina

I dedicate this book to all who seek the truth of our spiritual existence.

And, as always, to my wife Susan.

TABLE OF CONTENTS

FOREWORD vii

PART ONE: ACCELERATED EVOLUTION

1. The Journey Begins 3
2. Transition 13
3. Welcome Home 19
4. My New Life 23
5. Awakening. 29
6. My Decision 37
7. My Quest for Answers. 41
8. Entering the Second Heaven. 45
9. My Spiritual Training Begins 49
10. Recognizing the Power of the Mind 55
11. Creation Training. 63
12. The Power of Intention 75
13. Confronting my Fear 79
14. The River of Thought 81
15. The Cleansing 85
16. The Human Dreaming Fields 87
17. Anchored to the Past 93
18. Assisting a Transition. 97
19. Continuing Addictions 101
20. Individual Attachments. 107

21. Hells of the Mind 111

22. Creation is Art 119

23. Religious Territories. 123

24. Healing Environments. 131

25. Nonhuman Heavens 137

26. The Education of Soul through Matter 141

27. Embracing the Present Moment 147

28. The Filter of Heaven. 149

29. The Structure of the Multiverse 151

30. Spiritual Navigation. 155

31. Review: Heaven Is a State of Consciousness. 165

32. Preparation for Reentry. 169

PART TWO: PREPARE FOR YOUR ADVENTURE

1. The Purpose of the Physical Training Ground. 173

2. Evolution through Matter. 177

3. States of Consciousness in the Afterlife. 185

4. Developing your Creative Ability. 191

5. Observing your Thoughts 195

6. Techniques for Change 199

7. Spiritual Exploration Mindset 211

8. Facilitating an Enlightened Transition 217

9. Questions and Comments. 229

Final Thoughts 247

Glossary. 249

Diagrams 260

FOREWORD

Your entire life can be turned upside down with one word: cancer. In March 2011, I was diagnosed with stage-four cancer of the tonsil and lymph nodes. What followed was a seven-month ordeal involving two throat surgeries, chemotherapy, and six weeks of daily radiation treatment. This story is the result of my life-changing confrontation with mortality and the dramatic shifts in consciousness that accompanied the entire experience. During this intense personal challenge, there was a radical change in my waking and dream life while new visions of reality opened to me.

On every level, my life was drastically altered. For many months, I could consume only liquids, while sleep came in brief, thirty-minute respites. The throat pain from my surgeries was so intense I had to brace myself each time I swallowed. I began to journal my daily experiences to shift attention from the constant, grinding ache.

The burning question of what occurs after this life inspired my exploration of the afterlife. My lucid dreams and out-of-body experiences provided mind-bending visions that stunned me to the core. To the best of my ability, I have attempted to organize this flood of insight into a logical, linear format.

In part one you will experience my life through the eyes of Frank Brooks, a fictional character based on my own adventures in consciousness. Follow Frank on this journey and witness his death and initial entrance into a traditional religious reality. His need for self-knowledge propels him beyond the comfortable, belief-based heaven of his youth, where he discovers a spiritual training center designed for accelerated growth. With the assistance of highly evolved guides, he experiences a series of intense lessons that explore his multidimensional self and the unseen nature of our universe. He sets out on a daring quest to uncover the mysteries of the afterlife and discovers thought-responsive environments beyond his wildest imagination.

Part two presents information about our continuing adventures beyond the body and some easy-to-use methods to assist us in our individual journeys of consciousness. For many of us, the time has come to open our minds and explore the amazing reality of our multidimensional existence. Always remember that we are powerful creative beings who possess the ability to shape our current existence and also our continuing life beyond the physical world.

The purpose of this book is to provide insight into the spiritual path that lies before us. The more prepared we are, the greater our potential to accelerate our personal growth and navigate the many thought-responsive environments we will experience in the afterlife.

My hope is that this book will assist your journey in this life and the next.

All my best,
William

www.astralinfo.org.

PART ONE

ACCELERATED EVOLUTION

CHAPTER 1

THE JOURNEY BEGINS

JUNE 18, 2011

"Stage four, inoperable cancer …" is all that I hear. My mind locks.

As I walk out of the doctor's office, the news begins to sink in. I am only thirty-seven years old and I'm going to die. The bitter-green hospital walls seem to close in around me. I can't breathe, can't think. Trying to hold back the inevitable tears, I'm lost in a maze of winding hallways and endless swinging doors. Finally, I recognize one of the openings as an elevator and punch at the button as though it were somehow at fault. My ears are ringing and my throat has started to close. Focusing, I struggle to remember where I'm going, although it really doesn't seem to matter. The elevator jerks to a stop at the lobby and I aimlessly follow a group of people as they herd out of the building and onto the street. The noise of the city fades as I fumble for my cell phone and dial my wife. I need to hear her voice.

"The news isn't good," I tell her. "I'll be home soon." The analogy of going home doesn't occur to me right away.

Tracy is waiting on the front porch and gently takes my hand, whether to calm me or to hang on to what little time we have left together, I don't know. I admit it is comforting to know that she will be by my side during this ordeal. At her request, I decide to keep this journal; I hope it will help me gain some perspective on the remaining months of my life.

JULY 12, 2011

Doctors tell me that chemotherapy may prolong my life. The quality of that life is questionable, but I have to do it for my family. Anticipating my first treatment, I sit with Tracy in the dimly lit waiting room. My anxiety grows with every moment. A thin, older gentleman comes in and sits across from us. A sad-looking woman signs the register at the reception desk and takes the seat next to him. She watches as his name is called and he walks unsteadily toward the nurse. When he is out of earshot, the woman tells us that her father has a rare form of inoperable lung cancer and has been given less than six months to live. He is seventy-nine years old, a Vietnam veteran. She fights to hold back the tears as she tells us his story. The chemo treatments will give him only a five-percent chance to move beyond the six-month mark. I seriously wonder if I would endure the notorious side effects of chemo for only a five-percent improvement; I doubt it. Only then does it hit me that our situations are not all that different.

My name is called next and I am guided to a green vinyl recliner, where I will be seated for the next five hours. It is a strange, sterile environment with the constant sound of TV soap operas and game shows filling the room. Identical recliners line each wall, and patients sit hooked to their lifelines of clear, toxic-chemical bags. My fellow patients read, watch TV, or participate in discussions of family stories and their life situations. It's clear that the nurses have been through this a thousand times as they listen to the patients' stories, feigning interest. I observe my surroundings and feel completely disconnected from the unfolding events; it is as if I were watching a movie of someone else's life.

I'm surprised by how nauseated I feel after the treatment, and for several days I seriously wonder if it is worth it. But when I look at my little girls, I vow to do whatever it takes to fight this monster that is consuming my life.

AUGUST 27, 2011

I can't believe how fast my entire existence has spiraled downward, completely out of control. All my life, I've been strong and energetic, overflowing with drive and ambition. Now I can only watch as my body grows weaker with each passing day. Each breath is a chore. Sometimes I think it would be easier to give in, but then Maggie brings me her teddy bear to hold, thinking it will make me well again, or Lizzie asks if I can have cookies and juice with her, and I think maybe I can beat this and prove the doctors are wrong. I need to get stronger, but inside I know the wretched truth: each day is getting worse.

SEPTEMBER 4, 2011

My life has become a whirlwind of medical appointments. The doctors say my cancer has advanced and they don't appear hopeful that chemo will stop the spread. Deep inside, I've known for some time that this was a losing battle, but I've tried to stay positive for Tracy's sake.

For days, I prayed to God to spare me from this horror: "*Lord, I promise to be a better man if I'm healed of this nightmare.*" But in my heart, I know it is too late for deals.

Tonight is my last poker night with the guys. We've been playing every other week since I joined the firm over ten years ago. Even though they say they want me to stay, I can tell that watching me get weaker is not fun. The baseball caps I wear are a poor disguise for my balding head and in all fairness to the group I know it's time to leave the game.

OCTOBER 17, 2011

I have been unable to work since my chemo treatments began, and now it's becoming difficult to command my own limbs to move. This disease is devouring my body and I'm rapidly losing weight. Exhaustion overtakes me as I walk down the hall to the bathroom. The doctors and nurses tell me this is a normal process, but it feels as though an evil curse has been placed on my body. I find myself struggling to accept my body's relentless decline.

People say that everything has a purpose, but what could be the purpose for the daily weakening of my organs and the loss of the very memories I hold dear? Sometimes I have a hard time just remembering the names of my girls, Maggie and Lizzie, my little twin angels. They will start first grade next year, and I fear that I won't be there to hold their hands as they go to school for the first time. Every day begins with the dread of what will happen next.

Why would God allow this to occur? What have I done to deserve this?

OCTOBER 31, 2011

Today is Halloween. I recognize the irony as I watch children dressed as skeletons and ghosts. They are laughing and trading candy. I feel like one of the walking dead that the costumed children are impersonating.

NOVEMBER 12, 2011

I've read that the mysterious process of dying is natural. I'm reassured that there are predictable stages of psychological change and I'm told that eventually I will reach a final acceptance of this malicious decay that has spread through my body. What a load of crap. There is no acceptance, only anger. I can't find a single reason for this raging insanity. It's completely senseless that the cells of my own body have turned against me, consuming my life.

DECEMBER 1, 2011

I'm so very tired. Unanswered questions bore into my brain. What is the purpose for this fight to the death? Why would God allow this cellular heresy to exist? I've been a good Christian all my life; I've done the best I could. Why am I being punished?

DECEMBER 5, 2011

Pastor Clark visited me today. He read some Bible passages and tried his best to be supportive. "Make peace with your situation and trust the Lord," he said. It took all my strength to hold my tongue; my faith in miracles is in damn short supply. I didn't tell him, but all I really feel is a deep-seated anger that saturates every cell of my being. I feel abandoned by God.

DECEMBER 17, 2011

My body grows weaker with each passing day. With my wife's help I'm making it through the chemo treatments. The spreading cancer is eating my life away with shocking speed, and it feels weird to admit that a portable oxygen tank has become my friend and constant companion.

DECEMBER 25, 2011

Christmas is just sad. Family members visit and try their best not to appear shocked by my frail appearance. The awkward small talk, punctuated by poor attempts at humor, is exhausting. I just want all of them to leave. Their faces say it all and I feel like a freak in a bad circus act.

DECEMBER 31, 2011

Today is New Year's Eve. My big resolution is to breathe just one more day. I try my best to look comfortable so my wife won't fuss over me. She's amazing; I don't know how she does it but she always manages to smile.

I have slowly accepted my fate. If only I could see the big picture and know that there is some kind of great, unseen, cosmic plan at work. There must be a divine purpose behind all of this but for the life of me I don't see it.

JANUARY 3, 2012

As a withered shadow of my former self, my daily care has become a demanding chore. My wife is a warrior who has done the best she could to take care of me. I know I've become a terrible liability to my family. For several days I have suggested going to a place where professionals can take care of me. She refused at first but finally conceded after my repeated insistence.

JANUARY 7, 2012

Today I was taken to the hospice care center. As I was carried from my home to the waiting ambulance, a strange thought filled my mind: this will be the last time I will see my house? How many hours did we spend picking out the perfect shade of paint for the front door? The gardens are bare now, but I know that in the spring they will be alive with color. This was our dream home, the first house we bought together. Then it hit me that the idea of possessing anything is a complete illusion. Nothing can be owned. We arrive in and depart from this life with nothing. For the first time, I clearly see that the entire concept of ownership is a grand fantasy.

JANUARY 8, 2012

My room is comfortable; not that it matters much. Tracy visits me for much of the day, but I'm exhausted and sleep most of the time. She looks beautiful. I love my kids, but I will miss her more than anything. My doctor's liberal use of pain medicine doesn't ease my labored breathing and I grow tired of the endless fight. Drifting in and out of consciousness, I wake to a peaceful, floating sensation. *People surround the bed and gently touch me; they whisper my name, but the nurses don't seem to see or hear them. They are trying to comfort me. A voice says to me, "We are here with you."*

JANUARY 9, 2012

I struggle to focus as Tracy reads to me from the Bible. My favorite passage is Psalm 23, which I know by heart and recite silently as I drift to sleep: "The Lord is my shepherd; I shall not want. He maketh me to lie down in green pastures; he leadeth me beside still waters.

He restoreth my soul; he leadeth me in paths of righteousness for his name's sake. Yea, though I walk through the valley of the shadow of death, I will fear no evil; for thou art with me."

I'm dreaming. It's dark and I find myself wandering through an endless series of hallways, trying to find my body. I feel like a point in space desperately attempting to locate my physical form. Then it hits me—I must be dead. I'm jerked awake, my mind is racing. I thought I was dead, but I am still here. This convinces me that the end is near.

JANUARY 10, 2012

Light is streaming through the window as I steal each breath from the power that is death. For many months I've battled this cancer, and now I face the inevitable with a strange mix of fatigue and acceptance. This war is lost but my mind is clear. Vivid images from my childhood come alive and a newfound clarity wells from deep inside. There is a simple truth: I have wasted too much of my life focusing on the lifeless objects around me. All of the possessions I worked so hard to obtain are meaningless and only the love I hold is truly important. I have been so blind. Why did it take my impending death to understand something so basic? It's ironic that it took me to the end of my life to open my eyes and finally see what living should be.

My wife sits by my bed and it is all she can do to hold back the tears as she places my frail hand in hers. It breaks my heart to think that I might not see her again. I'm too weak to speak. I can't tell her how much I love her but I'm sure she knows. My precious little girls stand by the bedside, and I can see that Maggie is startled by my withered appearance; she touches my arm as tears trickle down her soft, perfect cheeks. Lizzie hides behind her mother, unable to even look at me.

Sadness wells up inside until I feel like I will burst. Tracy's hand is stroking mine, and then she's gone. I wish I had more time.

JANUARY 11, 2012, 2:00 A.M.

I'm jolted to awareness as a powerful buzzing sound and intense vibrations surge through me. *I feel weightless as I float away from my body. It's a wonderful sensation of freedom; no pain, no struggle for breath. Voices speak to me and I strain to comprehend the words. Several people feel close to me and even though their words are muffled; I clearly hear my name called. It must be the middle of night yet my room is illuminated by ethereal, silvery light.* Spontaneously, I think about my physical body and I'm instantly there, lying on the hospice bed. Damn. Once again I feel the heavy dull pain of my body.

CHAPTER 2

TRANSITION

JANUARY 12, 2012, 2:35 P.M.

As I drift in and out of consciousness, images of my life flash through my mind. I can't believe how fast my entire existence has passed by. In contrast, I recall how slowly the clock moved when I was a child waiting for Christmas morning to dawn. After going to evening church on Christmas Eve, we would ride around the neighborhood looking at the holiday lights. I can still smell the sweet-potato pie that my Aunt Sophie baked every year.

I find myself floating from one familiar life event to another. Coming into view is my teenage self in red swim trunks sitting on a tall, white stand at the community pool. At the age of sixteen, I was so proud to have passed all the rigorous tests to become a lifeguard. Before me there are vivid pictures from the day I pulled an unconscious, freckle-faced boy out of the deep end after he hit his head on the diving board. My CPR training was put to use until the ambulance arrived. They told me that I saved his life.

At the beginning of college, I didn't think I would ever make it to graduation. Four years seemed so far away, but as I see myself walking across the stage to accept my diploma I can only remember the confidence that my family always had in me. Tracy was there; I proposed to her later that evening. What a classy wedding, with flowers at each pew and garlands around the altar. There was a four-piece orchestra playing in the back of the church. I can hear the music now. I smile, thinking about how my bride wanted every detail to be perfect, and all I wanted was to have her as my wife.

Then we were blessed with our twin babies and I see the replay of their baptism in the same church. I've been so lucky to have these beautiful girls in my life, even for just a short period of time.

The last time I was in that chapel was to say goodbye to my mother. She worked so hard all of her life, it was almost a relief to see she was finally able to rest. I hope that she has found her reward in heaven.

Powerful vibrations surge through me, dragging me away from my visions. A peaceful light saturates my mind and all my fear dissolves away. I can scarcely tell what is real and what is shaped by the cool liquid that slowly drips into my veins.

There is no more pain. I hear voices around me and realize that my legs, which had been pressing against the sheets, now seem to be melting away. Is someone touching my hand? I can't tell for sure. Sparks are flowing up my arm; this tingling is something I've never felt before.

Then I hear music; the sound comes from both deep within and far in the distance. It's the chiming of bells and the clear tone of pure crystal singing to me. Again, there is a touch on my arm, a gentle stroking from my wrist and across the top of my hand to the end of my fingertips. My arm is drawn up to the ceiling, so light that it feels like it has detached from my body. I can only watch as my other arm begins the same journey. It has become an endless reach, searching for another world.

I can feel myself moving, yet my body is still. Are my senses deceiving me?

The smell of mint is unmistakable. I'm a child in my grandfather's garden, picking mint leaves and chewing slowly while the sunlight warms my face. I sit on the ground with my knees bent, my arms around my legs. The scent of mint would linger on my fingers for hours, but I can no longer feel my hands, so where is this sweet fragrance coming from? The music seems to be getting closer with each passing moment. The chimes have become the background to a host of perfect voices.

The words are indistinguishable but the sounds are soothing. It feels like I'm losing control of my body but I no longer care.

A warm glow engulfs my mind as a spreading lightness flows through me. I don't feel my body at all, now floating up and away from the arms and legs that bound me to the Earth. Fully conscious, I'm moving through a radiant tunnel of blinding light. It's beautiful. The sparkling energy cannot be described in words that I know. It softly wraps around me, filling my spirit with new life and clean, cool energy. In my imagination I could never have pictured this scene; it's a light not of our world. The radiance is pure—angelic in nature. The feeling of being loved is overwhelming as an aura of complete peace and harmony surrounds me.

Motion blurs my senses. I try to focus, adjusting to the brilliant light. It's as if I have been in a dark room for a long time and someone has just switched on the lights. My feet have feeling again and to my surprise, I'm standing. Disoriented but aware, I sense unseen beings around me. Their voices seem muffled; my surroundings unclear. As my vision improves, I begin to see the hazy outlines of people around me.

This new world comes alive and human forms begin to take shape. Images and sounds become sharper. People are laughing and hugging each other as joyous reunions fill my senses. One woman stands alone, waving a flag, and a young man in a military uniform quickly joins her. The connection between them is almost tangible. I turn and see a young boy; he seems lost until he is greeted by an older gentleman—his grandpa. They share warm smiles and a big hug as they become family again. They quietly walk away together, hand in hand. As I look around I sense that someone is here for me, too.

A familiar energy is close, and I strain to see the features of a young woman. I hear the comforting sound of a feminine voice calling my name: "Frankie." It's so clear. This is no dream; it's the voice of my mother.

Recognizing this loving sound, I struggle to verify the image before me. This woman has the same facial appearance as my mother but is much younger and thinner than I remember. She wears a yellow sundress with tiny red hearts. Her shining, dark hair and wide smile illuminate the space around her. She wraps her arms around me and squeezes me tightly; it takes my breath away. Her hug feels like a warm blanket of love and comfort.

To my surprise, her thoughts flow effortlessly into my mind: "I was surprised to hear that you were arriving so soon."

I don't take my eyes off of her, fearing she might disappear as quickly as she arrived. "Is this real? Am I dreaming?"

I sense her memorable laugh as she says. "Frankie, of course it's real."

Overwhelmed, I ask, "Is this heaven?"

"Welcome home." Her eyes say it all.

I look down at my legs and arms and realize that I'm standing; no more pain, no struggle for breath. As I touch each limb a wave of euphoria washes over me. I'm alive and I feel like I've been born again.

She smiles brightly. "We are all reborn in heaven."

My mother's youthful appearance amazes me. With long brown hair and glowing smile, she appears to be twenty-five years old. My memory of her as an elderly, overweight woman is shattered. She overflows with energy and seems to know my every thought. "Everyone can be young and healthy in heaven."

She takes my hand, and we communicate with our thoughts. It feels natural and effortless as her feelings and thoughts flow together through my mind. "Come with me." I turn for one last look at where I am, but the scenery has already melted away. She takes my hand and escorts me to a series of white archways.

She leads me through the arches and the change is dramatic; a vista of scenic, rolling hills, lush trees, and a vibrant green field extends as far as I can see. The light and colors are so intense I must stop for a moment so my vision can adjust. My mother smiles and says, "Your new body will quickly adapt."

CHAPTER 3

WELCOME HOME

In awe, I survey my new world. It appears to be the rolling green hills of western Maryland. Directly in front of me is a semicircle of red-brick, colonial-style houses, each with a white picket fence and slate stones leading to a covered front porch. The hand rails are gleaming and the flower boxes at each window overflow with a cascade of color. My mother beams with pride as she escorts me through the gate and up to the front steps. I scan the neighborhood as she points to a house down the street.

"Aunt Sophie lives over there."

"I wonder if she is still baking pies."

"Of course, and they are still delicious." I can sense that my mother is thrilled to finally live in the beautiful home that had eluded her during her physical life.

As we approach the front door, I notice that it's painted bright white with two small windows. An eight-inch, silver cross seems to float in the center. The inside of her home is spotlessly clean with plain furnishings, including a large, green sofa and a comfortable, brown recliner in the corner. The rooms have an inviting, warm feeling with a large, brick fireplace, wood trim, and an Early-American-style dining set.

My mother's thought fills my mind. "Life is perfect here." She guides me to an overstuffed, pale-green chair and says, "I know this is a big change for you; it's a lot to absorb."

We sit for a moment as I try to process my new surroundings. My mind is in overdrive. The awesome reality sinks in; I'm in heaven. The chemo, the nausea, and all the pain and hardships of the physical world are behind me. A wave of elation envelops me as I realize that I've finally made it home. I'm bursting with questions, but I find myself weak from the transition.

"We will have plenty of time to catch up; you must be exhausted." She senses my need to rest and escorts me down a hallway to an empty bedroom. As I enter, my childhood memories come alive. The walls are covered in blue wallpaper with narrow yellow stripes. My favorite childhood science-fiction movie poster, *The Day the Earth Stood Still*, appears next to a twin bed that is amazingly similar to the one I slept on when I was a young boy. On top of an old brown dresser sits the model of a World War Two Spitfire fighter plane that I built when I was ten years old.

"I've prepared a room that I thought you would enjoy," my mother says to me, recognizing my confusion.

"It's amazing," I say as I pick up a picture book and flip through the pages.

"I'm glad you like it." She pauses as I continue to examine my room. "The change is tiring; you should sleep now." She kisses my cheek and closes the door behind her. A wave of fatigue sweeps through me and I collapse on the blue-plaid comforter of my childhood bed. As I stretch out on the covers, my thoughts return to my wife and kids. How they are doing? How will Tracy be able to raise our children without any help from me? I desperately wish to see them again.

Closing my eyes, I feel an intense internal pull from the center of my torso. I'm rising up from my bed, parallel to the sheets. Just as quickly the location changes and I am standing in my daughters' bedroom. My little girls are sleeping in their twin beds. They look like precious angels. With a gentle kiss on their foreheads I whisper, "Daddy loves you more then you will ever know. I'm sorry I had to go away."

Maggie senses my presence and opens her eyes. "Daddy, are you OK now?"

"Yes, I'm much better."

"I'm sad."

"Don't be sad. I'm in heaven now with Grandma."

"When will I see you again?"

"It might be a little while, sweetie, but we'll be together again someday."

"I miss you."

"Be a big girl for your mother." I try to pull the blanket up under her chin.

"OK, Daddy. I love you."

A wave of pain sweeps through me. "I'll always love you."

"Who are you talking to, Maggie?" I hear Lizzie say in her sleepy voice.

"It's Daddy. He's all better now."

"I miss him."

"Me too, go back to sleep."

"OK. Good night, Maggie."

Maggie smiles and slips back to sleep.

I think about Tracy and I am suddenly standing next to her as she sleeps in our bed. She looks so beautiful. Sitting next to her, I run my fingers gently through her hair. I can't help but lean over slightly to kiss her lips. "I miss you."

She moans quietly and touches her mouth. "Frankie," she mumbles and rolls over.

I wonder if she will remember this moment.

CHAPTER 4

MY NEW LIFE

After sleeping for what seems like days, my eyes slowly open and there's an unfamiliar energy rushing through my body. Once fully awake, I feel more refreshed than I've felt in years. Gathering my thoughts, a sudden panic washes over me; *was the entire memory of entering heaven just a cruel dream?* Jumping out of bed, I stare at the full-length mirror attached to the back of the bedroom door. A young man looks back, and I know it's me. It's not a dream; I'm alive and full of energy again. My body is as light as a feather and I can see that I'm about twenty-five years old. For the first time in a long while, there is a head of thick, dark hair surrounding my young face in the mirror. I can't help but laugh aloud for I know it's real—this must be heaven. A surge of relief sweeps through me; I feel reborn.

The smell of fresh coffee and sound of sizzling bacon breaks my concentration and sends me to the kitchen. My mother is a burst of sunshine as she prepares her traditional Sunday breakfast. She turns to greet me with a smile and hands me a glass of freshly squeezed orange juice. My senses are heightened; every color and scent is so intense, I can even smell the sweetness of the juice.

As we talk over breakfast I quickly learn that there is an exciting world to discover. With so much to see and do, I'm eager to explore my new home, my new life here in heaven. I flood my mother with questions and am sometimes surprised by the answers. My mother's personality and sense of humor have remained remarkably unchanged. With a big smile she hands me a plate of bacon and eggs. While eating, I share my experience from the previous night.

"Last night I visited Tracy and the girls."

"That's good. Visiting loved ones is normal; most of us return to say goodbye right after our arrival. It's hard to let go of the ones we love."

"I was surprised that Maggie was aware of my presence."

"Some people are just more sensitive than others. Children are especially open," she said as she refilled my juice glass.

"So I will see them again?"

"Of course you will. And someday you may select a house for your family to live in, just as I have. Maybe right here in this neighborhood."

"How do you know this?" I ask as I continue to devour my breakfast.

"Because I visited you after I died. You might have remembered it as a dream."

"You're right. I do remember you in my dreams. It seemed so real."

"It was real, and here you are, at home again with me."

EXPLORING HEAVEN

My first weeks in heaven are devoted to exploring this world of endless beauty; spectacular waterfalls, pristine lakes, and stunning sunsets are a daily spectacle. Every tree, flower, and blade of grass seems vibrantly alive, creating a mesmerizing landscape. Each living thing glows with energy and life. I never realized so many colors were possible. Some of these breathtaking vistas are similar to places I visited in my old life, but everything here is enhanced beyond my comprehension.

At first it's overwhelming, for there is so much to discover. I'm finding that many of my old ideas and concepts are meaningless here. Since we don't age, time has little bearing on my daily life. Each day is highlighted by magnificent sunrises and sunsets that flow together with no thought of clocks or calendars.

For a few dozen of these sunrises, I live with my mother. She is wonderful, helping me adapt to my new life; we spend many evenings sitting on the front porch talking about the wonders of heaven. She likes to discuss the recent arrivals—how they died and where they will live in heaven. But eventually it's time for me to select my own home. I have decided to stay in this neighborhood, but I choose a house with a more modern feel.

It is comforting to know that heaven is every bit the paradise that I imagined it would be. Most of the people here are busy pursuing their creative interests while others are studying the Bible. I often see people in the parks enjoying picnics, painting, and playing all kinds of sports while the sound of inspirational music can be heard everywhere.

As I stroll through the beautiful commons, I frequently stop to admire the artists as they create colorful landscapes. They seem to radiate intense hues of light and color not found on Earth. Heaven is so vast that no one has seen it all. A mountain range frames the west while an ocean creates the eastern border. One popular beach is famous for its magnificent sand sculptures, incredible creations portraying important events in the Bible. They are so detailed that they appear to come to life.

Most people live in small communities with beautiful white churches located at their centers. With wide sidewalks radiating outward, these churches are the focal points of all major social activity. Individual homes are similar to each other; they are about the same size with white picket fences, muted colors, large windows, and wide front porches. Even though I've never seen anyone cutting the grass, the yards and hedges are always emerald green and perfectly manicured. Each home has an array of flowers in the yard, window boxes overflowing with color, and a shining silver cross on the front door. The neighborhoods I've visited project a distinct feeling of comfort, peace, and sanctuary.

Every Sunday morning we attend church and praise our Lord. Our pastor imparts passionate sermons that are truly inspirational. He seems to know every verse of the Bible from memory and brings the biblical stories to life. Everyone respects him.

During church services, we thank God for the miraculous gift of our eternal life and our acceptance into his heavenly kingdom. We sing hymns of joy and praise, and I'm always inspired when I witness so many moved to tears as they worship our savior. Our choir sings "Amazing Grace" with such power that the entire church seems to vibrate. Every week, several in our congregation are so overwhelmed by the rapture they collapse in ecstasy.

Each week I attend regular church functions, where we discuss the Gospels and the works of the lord. We also have weekly socials, dinners, prayer circles, and even dances. Various church discussion groups offer Bible readings and explore the word of God in detail. Several people I know are experts on specific books of the Bible and can repeat the entire text from memory.

As I explore this world of peace and harmony, I realize that no atheists or false religions are found in heaven. We all share the same beliefs and are told by our pastor that we're the chosen of God. I imagine that the nonbelievers must be in some dreadful place. I don't dwell on it; a hellish existence is just too terrifying.

QUESTIONING REALITY

Every Sunday after church, I visit my mother's home for lunch. We talk about everything, but a few things trouble me. "Where are Jesus and the disciples? Why are so many of our dead friends and relatives on Earth not with us?" Even my childhood pastor and my father are not here. I've asked a lot of people this question and I always get the same response: "Only God knows. Trust in the Lord."

The following week after church, I present my questions to the pastor, and he appears to be annoyed. "Frank, God has placed us in his heavenly world as a reward for our unwavering faith. Have faith, for we are being prepared for the presence of the Lord."

During a weekday church social, I politely ask one of the senior church matrons a question. "If we're the chosen, why isn't Jesus here with us?"

Her face turns red as she reprimands me. "My child, do not question our Lord. It's blasphemy."

Shocked by her serious demeanor, I respond meekly. "Sorry, I didn't mean to offend anyone."

"You are weak of faith, young man. The pastor will hear of this." Her voice fills the meeting hall as she glares at me. Everyone at the gathering stops as I retreat from the awkward situation. This is not what I expected; instead of finally obtaining answers, I'm repeatedly told to have faith. With every passing day, more questions fill my mind. Where are the angels? Is this really heaven? What is this place?

I'm struck by the realization that many of these people have lived here for decades of Earth time and they still don't possess a single answer to the basic questions of our existence. This is not what I expected in the afterlife.

Surely someone in heaven must have the answers.

CHAPTER 5

AWAKENING

Every day my questions grow and even my dreams seem to fuel my search for answers. During sleep I sometimes feel strange vibrations and hear loud sounds that startle me. One night, I felt as if I was wide awake during a vivid dream.

I become fully aware while walking down a lighted, narrow path. At first, I'm moving merrily along, but I quickly realize that dirty trashcans are blocking my way. I instinctively begin to push and kick the trash cans away from my path. With each step the battered trashcans become heavier and more difficult to move until they completely block my way. Feeling overwhelmed I become light-headed and begin to lose consciousness. Vibrations surge through me and I find myself floating up from my body. A wave of fear hits me and with a jolt I'm slammed back into my body and open my eyes.

My entire body was paralyzed for a moment as I tried to comprehend what had occurred. I couldn't sleep and stayed up for hours trying to figure out what was happening to me. The next night as I was drifting off to sleep, I heard a deafening buzzing sound.

I can see through my eyelids and again my body is paralyzed, prompting a wave of intense anxiety. I float upward out of my body and as I struggle to get my bearings, a soft female voice speaks to me, "When you are ready, the answers will appear."

Upon hearing the voice, I immediately fell back into my body. My mind is in overdrive. What was this? The feminine voice sounded so familiar. I remember hearing this melodic tone before my death. Sleep is impossible as I try to make sense of these strange experiences.

CONFRONTATION

The following Sunday, after the regular church services the pastor takes my arm and escorts me to a back room. As he sits me in a corner chair; his left hand gently rests on my shoulder. In his other hand he clutches a worn Bible close to his chest. His voice is filled with emotion.

"Frank Brooks, I'm disappointed in you. Doubting the word of our Lord is a serious matter." He scowls at me looking for some response, but I don't know what to say. His voice trembles as he continues.

"You must pray for forgiveness. Become steadfast in your faith."

I think the pastor is trying to help me in his own way, but it is not working. Out of respect, I try to respond with a cool head. "What's wrong with seeking answers, with searching for the truth?"

"Our Lord has no need for a disbeliever who contaminates the chosen flock. Obey the scriptures and pray to God for His mercy. Now go home and think about what I've said today."

As I slowly walk away from the church, I can't help but wonder. Why are logical questions so threatening? How can all these people be content without any answers? How can they go day after day living in this limbo? Now, more than ever, I'm driven to discover the truth of heaven and myself.

INTERVENTION

A few days later, I'm invited to my mother's house for a home-cooked meal and, to my surprise, there are a dozen church members and the pastor milling around the living room. This is no dinner party and I quickly discover they have gathered to participate in my religious intervention. The preacher unleashes his booming church voice while some of the matrons are lighting candles.

"Mr. Brooks, you are in the midst of a grave emergency. You have lost your faith and your immortal soul is in danger." He nods to a man across the room as a signal to begin playing the organ.

My first reaction is, "You must be kidding." I think about bolting out of the house, but I try to be patient as they pull a chair to the center of the room. Reluctantly, I sit as the music fills the room.

"Listen to me, Frank Brooks. You must follow the word of our Lord," the pastor continues his lecture.

My so-called friends encircle me in the living room and slam me with non-stop scripture. I can't believe my ears. To make things worse, the pastor leads the chorus. The entire group chimes in, berating me for questioning my faith.

"Trust in the word of our Lord and you will be saved."

"Cast out your evil thoughts and accept the Lord."

"Repent your sins, young man." An angry, older man I've never met shakes a dog-eared Bible in my face. A woman I barely know is praying quietly to herself while another glares at me and repeats the same sentence: "The word of God is our rock and our salvation."

They begin to sound like crazed parrots spouting the same rehearsed lines. I struggle to remain composed, but after this barrage I respond, "Why is seeking the truth a sin? If this is heaven, where's Jesus?"

"Believe in the Lord." In response, the distraught assembly explodes, waving their hands in the air.

"Have faith in the Bible."

"Cast out the sinful spirit."

My mother stands quietly in the back of the room, tears filling her sad eyes. I feel bad that I've disappointed her but I can take no more of this and storm out of the house. The organ music begins to fade as I hear my mother's pleading voice.

"Frankie, it's only because we love you," and the door slams behind me.

As I walk home, I ponder my strange situation. How could this have happened? Why are logical questions so threatening? For the sake of my mother, I controlled my mouth most of the time, but I couldn't take their badgering any more. How can these people remain content without answers? Why are we here? What is this so-called heaven? I'm sure that Jesus himself would demand the answers if he were here.

I can't believe they ambushed me. The entire group sounded like programmed robots, and it was obvious the pastor enjoyed leading the entire, demeaning drama. I'm not sure how, but maybe this experience will turn out to be a blessing. One thing is certain: heaven will never be the same for me.

In a daze, I round the corner and climb the steps to my home.

SEEKING THE TRUTH

After the intervention, my church days are placed on indefinite hold but my desire for answers expands with each passing day. All of my church friends and their warm invitations to the lunch socials suddenly disappear. Many of the people I meet on the street are now cold and distant; some are superficially polite but most just avoid me whenever possible. Occasionally I see someone pointing at me and then turning away in disgust. Heaven suddenly has a real chill in the air. To the dismay of my mother, I have become a social outcast.

My failed intervention is now common knowledge and, to my surprise, several people who also harbor hidden questions about their life in heaven begin to seek me out. Taking the initiative, I invite a few people to my home to discuss our shared concerns. We begin meeting once a week to discuss the many mysteries of our existence. Several burning questions always surface: where are we, why are we here, and what's next? If this is heaven, then where is Jesus? We are all tired of hearing the same old line, 'Have faith.' If we are truly in heaven, the answers should be here.

Each week our secret group meetings grow larger. We gather discreetly in different places where we can maintain some degree of privacy. Our discussions are always thought-provoking and though we often disagree, we respect each other's ideas. To keep us on track, I created a few basic guidelines; these include allowing each person to openly speak his or her mind and the importance of remaining open-minded to new ideas and viewpoints.

Our late-night gatherings become surprisingly intense. Ideas of religious heresy, damnation, and sin are often thrown into the mix. The questions are endless. Would God punish us for seeking the truth? What and where is God? After several lengthy debates, we jokingly name our group *The Heretics*. Our goal is to seek the truth, to obtain the answers of our existence. No subject is off limits.

We have so many questions, and as one member of our group states, "Why would God give us the free will to question things if he didn't want us to use it?" We focus on ways to obtain genuine insight and self-knowledge. The suggestions are diverse. Some consider logic, dreams, and various rituals, while others think the answers are found through intense daily prayer or altered states of consciousness.

"Jesus states, 'There are many mansions in my father's house,'" notes Jack, my last remaining friend from the church. He speaks while holding his well-worn Bible up for everyone to see.

"Maybe these mansions are other realities of the universe," I add.

"This is heaven, the Bible tells us," Jack says, returning to his Bible.

I'm beginning to wonder why Jack is here as I continue my thought. "Are we in heaven or just a reality we don't yet comprehend? Maybe there are millions of heavenly places, just as there are millions of planets in the physical universe."

Markus responds, "We're not in heaven; I think we're living in a pleasant form of purgatory, like a halfway house."

Several agree, "This could explain why we remain separated from the answers."

"Maybe Jesus lives in a higher region of heaven, and it's up to us to become better people by daily prayer, self-sacrifice, and good deeds," Julia says.

"I think we exist in a thought-created matrix, but we're too primitive to understand the energy source that maintains our environment," adds Joey.

Talia generally has a different take on our situation. "Maybe, everything we do here is a test of our faith."

Several nod in agreement. Sitting against the wall is Shiloh, a new member of our group. She hasn't participated in our discussions yet, but she listens with interest, occasionally nodding her head or smiling. I feel that she has something to say but isn't ready to share.

"It's possible we're in this heaven because we hold some doubts," Brad suggests in between mouthfuls of snacks.

Several group members shake their heads no. "I think we're living in a powerful hologram and we're subconsciously creating our environment with our thoughts," Robert says as he places a smokeless pipe in his mouth. He has a few converts to his ideas, but most people in the group think he's a little crazy. "After all, if our thoughts created this reality, why can't our thoughts create the answers and allow us to meet Jesus face to face?"

Judy thinks our world is a pleasant but artificial maze or zoo. "Maybe we're in an intergalactic research project." She takes off her glasses and stands to emphasize her point." We could be research subjects placed in an artificial three-dimensional environment being studied by some advanced species. It's said that highly advanced technologies always appear as magical or religious when introduced to a primitive culture." It's an interesting idea, but most people don't buy her science-fiction theory.

A normally quiet member of our group stops knitting long enough to shock everyone with a single statement. She speaks softly." Maybe Jesus is but a man seeking the truth about God, just like we are." The room becomes silent. This kind of speculation has never been expressed out loud.

Jack stands up and firmly says, "You guys are crazy. I'm out of here. You crossed the line; I'm not going to hell because of you idiots." He storms out of the house.

Alarmed by the direction of our discussion, we promptly end our meeting but agree to continue the following week. One by one, each person quietly gathers his or her belongings and heads to the door. Shiloh is the last to leave. She finally makes a comment that only I can hear. It's the first time I have seen her speak, but I know that voice. "I believe in you. Have faith in your intuition." Her thick, black hair glows and almost seems to have a light source of its own. I gaze into her deep violet eyes and think that in another lifetime, I might have found her to be attractive.

After the meeting I think about the situation. So much for open-minded discussion, we're more walled in by our attitudes than I had imagined. We haven't broken free at all. How can we move forward when we continue to embrace the past?

There's one thing we all agree on: we're in trouble if the church finds out about our little band of free thinkers. It's well known that questioning the official beliefs is a serious offense, maybe even a sin. Could we be cast out of heaven if the church discovers our group?

With each passing day I feel like I'm living in a place where everyone repeats the same weekly rituals and blindly follows the old programming without ever questioning why. It's amazing how the critical queries of our existence are pushed aside with one simple word: believe. I now see that this reality is a reflection of the physical world, and just like on Earth, most people will follow the established rules and then hope for the best. I can't live like this.

CHAPTER 6
MY DECISION

My personal experiences are becoming stranger by the day. During sleep I often experience intense vibrations and high energy sounds. Upon waking I remember vivid dreams of traveling to different places and experiencing a wide variety of people and environments. Sometimes these experiences are shockingly real. But last night my entire reality was shaken to the core.

I feel intense vibrations, then lightness. In shock I realize I'm floating away from my body and standing in the corner of my bedroom, looking at my sleeping body. I'm fully awake and my mind is in overdrive, desperately attempting to make sense of this wild new experience. Then I witness another soul—a petite being with a subtle glow and soft voice—who appears to be observing my actions. The visitor speaks to me through my thoughts. "When you are ready, you can explore beyond the confines of your body. You can obtain the answers you seek."

My body is immobile and, after a moment, I slowly begin to move my arms and legs. My mind surges with excitement. *What happened?* It was real: I actually separated from my body and entered a different world. I must reexamine everything I believe about my entire reality. I thought I was in heaven and my body was my soul, but something far more profound is the truth. Sleep becomes impossible; my mind is on fire as I journal the details of this intense experience.

At the next meeting, I excitedly share my experience. To my surprise, several people in the group respond that they have had similar experiences but are too mystified to talk about it; it is just too strange to accept.

For me, the revelation is clear: there must be other heavens or dimensions and people like me must live there. Even more mind-expanding is the realization that we can actually leave our bodies and visit these other realities. A higher level of discussion explodes within the group. An exciting new world has opened. Imagine if we can visit other heavens and communicate with the inhabitants of other realities. Everything we believe needs to be completely reap-praised. I feel like a door to the truth is finally opening, and I must discover more.

At our group's next meeting, I present some new ideas, "Is it possible that everything we have been told is flawed? Maybe it's up to each of us to seek the truth beyond this world."

Talia responds, "Now that I think about it, Jesus, John the Baptist, and many others were murdered for stepping out of line with the established beliefs of their day. They dared to question the religious establishment and paid the ultimate price."

We continue our discussion late into the night.

LEAVING HEAVEN

Even with the stimulating group discussions, I grow tired of the mind-numbing indoctrination that surrounds me. I feel like an alien in a strange, dysfunctional world. The sheer number of people who continue to settle for unconfirmed ideas amazes me.

After many days of deep contemplation, I decide to seek the answers beyond this place. My friends think I'm crazy; no one has ever walked away from the comfort and security of heaven. My departure is supposed to be a secret, but somehow word begins to spread. At my final weekly group meeting several members are shocked and visibly dismayed that I intend to leave.

"Have you lost your mind? No one leaves heaven. What do you hope to discover?" Markus appears surprisingly upset.

Robert takes his pipe out of his mouth long enough to add his opinion. "Explore here with us and we'll be part of your journey."

"Why leave? What can you possibly gain from doing this?" Judy asks. The outpouring of emotion is unexpected.

"You can't go. You're the leader of our group, the voice of reason; we need you here. Who will direct the meetings?" Brad's voice quivers.

"Frank, you should follow your inner guidance. You don't belong here and you know it." Shiloh silences everyone with her words of encouragement. It is the first comment she has made for all to hear, and I appreciate her support.

"I'm convinced that the answers must exist beyond this heaven," I hug each member and say my goodbyes.

The two things I will miss the most are my mother and the people in this group. As I pack some supplies for my expedition, my mother quietly watches. I give her a warm hug and promise that I will be back as soon as possible. She knows that I might not return, but she's too choked up to speak.

CHAPTER 7

MY QUEST FOR ANSWERS

I ready myself for this journey into the unknown. Since souls remain together in their comfortable villages, there is little information about the outer areas of heaven. No one that I know has explored or charted the uninhabited regions, so the size and terrain of heaven remain a mystery. Having seen the vast ocean that creates the eastern boundary, I decide to begin my exploration to the west. With much anticipation I begin my quest. I know the answers are out there and I'm confident that I'll discover them. No roads are present to guide me, so I must follow my intuition.

For what feels like an eternity I walk toward the setting sun, crossing hills and lush green valleys until I find myself facing a desert that extends to the horizon. It's an endless sea of pale white sand. I don't see or hear a living thing; I encounter only the raw wind and the ever-shifting sands. Trekking along the edge of the harsh wasteland I realize that time has no meaning here; everything is now. With every moment, I'm learning to embrace my journey and release the past. My destination is unknown and I grow to realize that the present moment is all I truly possess. Still I demand some form of resolution, for the journey has become an endless dream. Sometimes I feel like a detective searching for clues in the dark for my quest has become a long and lonely exploration.

Snow-covered mountains form the northern-most boundary of heaven. According to the religious elders these peaks are impenetrable, but I don't believe anything I've been told, especially since no one has attempted to travel through this desolate wilderness. I wonder what is on the other side, perhaps another heaven is waiting for me.

For what feels like endless weeks, I seek an opening through the mountains but find only jagged walls of stone blocking my path. My exploration has become an arduous search for answers, and I grow tired. With each day my progress becomes increasingly difficult as I claw my way through narrow ravines and steep valleys. Searching for something I don't fully understand, at every sunrise I hope to find a clue that will provide some insight. Exhausted, I collapse in a deep and barren stone gorge, embracing the rare luxury of sleep. I drift off to the eerie sound of the wind echoing through the rock formations.

I awaken in a dream and I'm climbing the steep side of a mountain. With great effort, I pull myself up to a stone ledge. Glancing down, I see a broad, green valley and a winding river far below. Turning, I witness a strange sight: a single bush covered in small, purple flowers growing directly out of a wall of solid gray rock. It looks surprisingly healthy and strong, and its vibrant color draws my attention. I wonder how it's possible for any living thing to grow out of a wall of solid stone. As I focus on this unusual sight, I become even more focused.

My thoughts are clear and I see everything around me. I'm totally awake, yet I know my body is asleep. The thought, 'I'm conscious,' explodes through my mind. A wave of excitement washes over me as I cry out, "I'm aware!" I'm fully conscious and standing next to my sleeping self. The reality is overpowering; I'm experiencing another form of myself. I compose my racing thoughts and examine my new body and surroundings; I appear the same but feel lighter, more energetic. Next to me I see the purple bush and instinctively know that it's far more than it appears; it's a conscious being.

Spontaneously I shout, "I need answers!"

The bush glows brighter and radiates a clear stream of thought. "You are the path you travel." It seems to anticipate my every question. The communication is a series of precise images. "The answers are not found in the outer worlds of form."

Frustrated, I respond, "I need answers, not riddles."

"The answers are not found in the facade of heaven."

I don't understand. "What do you mean by 'facade?' I'm in heaven."

A single thought slices through my mind: "Are you?"

"If this isn't heaven, what is it?"

"Form is the filter for heaven. You must go inward to know reality."

"Inward? What do you mean?"

With a jolt, I'm slammed back into my body and I regain awareness on the cold stone. My body feels numb, out of sync, and I can barely move. I slowly sit up and try to wrap my mind around this strange encounter. My eyes scan the granite cliff face in search of the purple bush, but all I see are vertical walls of solid stone; nothing could possibly grow here.

What was this? It was no dream. The communication was precise, like a surgeon's scalpel cutting into my brain. The word 'facade' echoes through my mind. If this entire heaven is just a simulation, then all of humanity is deceived on a biblical scale. The thought is too shocking to accept. What would be the purpose? It can't be true.

I desperately try to comprehend this revelation. "Form is the filter for heaven."

This is not what I expected. I'm seeking answers and instead discover more questions.

CHAPTER 8

ENTERING THE SECOND HEAVEN

After days of contemplation, I realize that searching for the answers to my existence in the outer world is hopeless. In deep meditation, I open to insight and answers.

I lose consciousness for a moment and when I regain awareness, my body is paralyzed but my mind is clear. I feel vibrations and surrender to a high energy sensation that saturates my body and mind. Remaining calm I effortlessly separate from my body; it's a powerful sensation of amazement and liberation. What's happening to me? As I scan my surroundings I'm startled by the strange sight before me; I'm standing next to my own body. My God, I'm experiencing an entirely new spiritual form. My mind struggles to grasp the reality before me; my old body appears dull and lifeless, but I feel energized, lighter. I examine myself and can see and feel that I still have density and a physical-like form. As I adapt to my new energy body, a sphere of light appears and a peaceful loving light envelopes my mind. I'm immediately reassured by this comforting presence. Warm thoughts fill my mind; the communication is precise, like rapidly unfolding images rather than words.

"Welcome."

"Where am I?"

"You have entered another dimensional reality."

I stare at the entity before me, trying to understand. For some reason I feel at ease in this new environment and safe in the presence of this soul. Questions flood my mind and I can barely control my excitement.

"Is this another heaven?"

"You may call it that, if you like."

"You mean there are many heavens?"

The being seems amused by my question, "More than the grains of sand on a beach."

"Who are you?"

"I am here to assist you on your continuing journey."

The gentle voice feels familiar.

"Where am I?"

"You have entered a reality for souls ready to see beyond their eyes. The real question is not about where you are. It's more like what you are."

The sphere of light slowly takes a human form. In amazement I watch as the form of a woman with piercing violet eyes and a familiar smiling face appears before me. I feel relieved. The soul before me is Shiloh, from my discussion group. Her very presence calms me; even so, my mind overflows with questions.

"What is this place? How did I get here?"

"Your search for answers has led you to a spiritual training reality; a school to explore and discover yourself."

"I have so many questions and I've been seeking answers for so long."

Shiloh smiles, "The answers to your questions are available if you are ready to open your mind."

"Yes, I am."

"Are you ready to release all the attachments you hold?"

"Yes, I've never been more ready."

My excitement grows and I try to calm myself.

"What advice can you give me?"

The answer comes quickly: "Embrace change."

I'm instantly swept off of my feet by a powerful force and transported to a completely different environment. The motion is intense.

CHAPTER 9

MY SPIRITUAL TRAINING BEGINS

I shield my eyes from the blinding light and vibrant energy surrounding me. My legs are wobbly. I recognize blurred forms around me and grasp the solid trim of a doorway until my balance returns. As my vision adjusts to the transition, I can see that I'm standing in what appears to be a high school classroom. A constant glow streams in through the many windows along one wall, filling the room with a soft, ethereal light. I notice a dozen people seated at desks; they appear to be young adults around my age, both male and female. I can sense their nervousness as they quietly talk among themselves and shift uncomfortably in their seats.

Some of the faces look familiar, but I can't place them. No one acknowledges me as I take a seat at the back of the class. There's a strange energy in the air. I feel apprehensive and decide to keep a low profile.

A petite young woman wearing a flowing, bright-orange robe enters the classroom with measured steps. She stands in front of us with a stiffness that suggests to me that she is not comfortable in her own body. With short, dark hair, pale green eyes, and a fragile appearance, she is all business as she scans each member of the class. Her communication is in the form of rapid thought images that saturate my mind.

"Do you know why you're in this class?"

No one responds as she silently examines each member of the group. The intensity of her stare makes me even more uneasy as her thoughts scan my mind.

"You have entered this reality because you are ready to awaken." She pauses and makes eye contact with each of us. "You suffer from a deep amnesia. You have forgotten what you are, your purpose, where you come from, and where you are going. You have wandered for many lifetimes in the outer worlds."

She examines each of us before continuing. "Recently, all of you have returned from the training reality that you call Earth. Every aspect of your mind has been polluted by your exposure to this dense energy." She stops for a moment, and I can feel her mind pressing on me. It's a strange probing sensation. "I sense that some of you have doubts about your need to attend this class." She pauses and appears to look through us.

"This class will be difficult for many of you. I expect your undivided attention. All of you have volunteered for this training and those who wish to leave can do so now."

No one moves.

"Be prepared. To use an Earth phrase, this is a training camp for developing souls," she glances around the room with steely eyes and says, "and I am the director." Her eyelids close and she gently dips her head in our direction. My anxiety grows. Suddenly her thoughts flood though my mind.

"During your many visits to Earth, each of you has chased self-made delusions. Lifetime after lifetime, you created a series of dramas, and even worse, you've blamed others for your issues. Your destructive habits and your lack of personal responsibility will cease with this class. From this moment, there will be no more excuses for the energies you create in your lives. Now let us begin. Clear your mind."

A panoramic vision of human history unfolds before me. I witness an endless series of wars and conflict as massive armies are locked in bloody battles over land, religions, and resources. The flags change, but the insanity remains the same. War after war develops before me. There are far too many to count. The horror is unspeakable: murder, torture, and man's inhumanity to his fellow man reaching back through time itself. I'm disgusted by the barbaric vision before me and attempt to turn away, but cannot. The images are burned into my mind as the director's thoughts jolt me back to the classroom.

"You have assimilated into a primitive species that has a long history of extreme violence and self-destruction; these beings have murdered billions of their own kind. You have become ensnared in the collective group insanity you call the human race. As a result, you have imprisoned yourself in the outermost regions of the universe." The director stops for a moment to make eye contact with a few in the front row.

"Many of you underestimate the great task before you. The physical illusions are so deeply entrenched that most humans never recognize the extent of their dysfunction. Now open your mind."

I'm lifted from my body by the power of the director's thoughts. The dramatic change startles me. A remarkable vision appears before me; I visit my past life from a new perspective. Memories come alive and like a movie I clearly see my past physical home, my family and my daily routine, as well as every object and possession I thought was needed to have a full life. My thoughts are transparent; I believe I am my body, my personality, my ego; I think I am my mind, my gender, race and nationality. I believe I am the many physical roles I have played: father, son, and husband. My entire self-identity is completely centered on my brief existence in matter. The director's thoughts reluctantly pull me from my revelation.

"All of you have experienced intense physical indoctrination while visiting Earth. From birth you were conditioned to accept a host of falsehoods without question. It's no wonder that billions of humans remain trapped in the outermost dimensions of the universe. As long as souls cling to the physical, they will continue to be separated from their spiritual essence—left to roam the lower worlds."

I immediately understand that I've allowed my physical self-identity to dominate my consciousness and alter my entire perception of reality. My growth has been blocked by my attachment to fleeting physical things and my obsession with the past. How can I ever hope to know the truth of my existence while stuck in this ever-changing labyrinth of form? The realization leaves me dazed. I'm caught in a trap of my own making.

Several students appear traumatized as the vision of their past lives unfolds before them. Shaken by their personal visions, someone blurts out, "Is this hell?"

"This is far worse because earthbound souls create this reality for themselves. They don't see that their repeated struggles in matter are self-created."

The entire class is silent. Finally, someone in the back of the room asks, "How can anyone escape this perpetual reincarnation?"

"The first step is to recognize your situation and the need for change. Eventually, humans grow tired of the dense illusions and seek spiritual enlightenment."

I turn to see a woman shaking her head. "This is brutal. There must be a better way."

"Awakening is essential."

I think to myself, *this will take forever.*

Our teacher's response is immediate: "All are immortal; the time that evolution may take is meaningless."

For the first time, I see the overwhelming amount of work that lies before me.

CHAPTER 10

RECOGNIZING THE POWER

OF THE MIND

The director scans my thoughts and continues, "Be aware, you will experience a series of intense lessons. The heavy residue of your past physical programming must be purged before you can progress. Now open your mind to a shift in your awareness." My eyes close and once again I feel myself lifted from my body.

Suddenly, I'm standing in a shallow pool of vibrant, liquid energy. There is power in this place. Before me is a magnificent waterfall of cascading, crystalline, silver-blue liquid. I'm drawn in and without hesitation step into the waterfall of glowing energy. The liquid saturates my mind and cleanses my body. It feels incredible; I'm noticeably lighter as vibrational currents of liquid light massage every aspect of my being.

I hear the director's thoughts, "Adjustments are being made to your energy body. Now you are ready to begin your training."

My vision expands, and I can clearly observe my past life on Earth. I watch myself pursuing the constantly changing desires of my mind; I can't believe how much of my life was consumed chasing the whims of my ego. I see myself in a dozen situations defending my entrenched views about politics, religion and every imaginable subject. I always thought I was open-minded, but now I know the bitter truth: I was completely programmed and resisted new ideas. As I observe my past physical life unfold I realize that my entire experience on Earth was just a brief, passing drama designed to educate me. If I had known the truth and opened my mind, I would have been a different man.

After this experience, I understand the pervasive power of my physical conditioning and I'm deeply disappointed with myself. Why didn't I see this earlier? My comfortable self-image is shattered and for the first time I see that I'm not the highly evolved soul that I believed myself to be.

With a shudder I'm returned to the classroom and see that the entire group appears to be in deep shock. Some are crying, while others appear bewildered.

Sensing our distress, the director says, "Being aware of your physical indoctrination is the first step to freedom from it. In this class, you will learn to take complete responsibility for your every thought and action."

She stops and waits for the group to calm themselves. After a pause she scans each member of the class as a single question fills my mind. "What is real?" Her piercing gaze moves to each student as she waits for a response, but no one moves. She lifts her hand and a large red apple appears. "Is this real?"

The class responds with nods of yes. The apple instantly changes to a plump yellow pear. "Is this real?" The group is silent. The pear dissolves from view and the apple reappears. "Which one was real?"

Finally, a woman seated in the back row speaks up. "Neither is real."

"Why?"

Someone in front meekly responds, "Because you created it?"

The class sheepishly nods in agreement. The instructor holds out her hands to reveal two red apples. She casually takes a bite and tosses the fruit to students in the front row.

"Taste it." The students are slow to react. The instructor insists, "Taste it now."

The two students holding the apples comply.

The question is repeated: "Is it real?" The students appear intimidated and awkwardly nod in agreement. The teacher presses harder. "Why is it real?"

A young man in the front row clears his throat and bravely says, "Because we touched and tasted it."

"You think things are only real if you can taste and feel them?"

The rest of the class meekly responds yes.

She confronts the class again. "Am I real? What am I?"

A woman in the back says, "You're a female soul."

The instructor smiles and abruptly changes into to a tall, muscular male with a dark beard with the same pale green eyes. The class is startled by the transformation. A deep, booming male voice asks, "What am I? Am I real? "

"You are a soul," a student responds.

"What is soul?" The class is quiet. In an instant the instructor's male body dissolves from view and a radiant orb of glowing white light appears before us. Powerful thoughts slice into my mind.

"The projection of form has nothing to do with what we are. What am I now?"

The class remains silent. The director reappears before us as the short, frail woman we first met. "Don't be deceived by the outer expressions of soul. All form is but the instrument and vehicle of consciousness." She pauses for a moment and scans the class. A holographic sketchpad appears before each of us. The device looks like a modern computer tablet and I wonder what she will ask us to do.

"This will magnify your thought energy." She lifts her hand, and a bright red apple appears. "Now focus and create an apple with your mind. Close your eyes and direct your undivided attention. Visualize the details—the shape, color, weight, and texture. Make it as detailed as you can. See and feel it with your mind. Concentrate. Vividly imagine and feel the fruit before you."

A few moments pass. I open my eyes and can't help but smile when I see a plump red apple before me. I look around and see the fruit on the desks of everyone in the class.

"Now, taste your creation. Is it real?" I take a bite of the apple as the instructor continues, "All the forms you experience in your life are created by the same, focused, thought process. During your physical life you were deceived by the illusions of form. This is a common error, for the density of matter slows the thought-creation process."

The electronic device before me dissolves from view. "You require no external aid to create your reality. Now close your eyes and clearly imagine an arrangement of flowers before you." The group complies and within moments colorful bouquets of flowers appear. I open my eyes and smile as I touch and smell the sweet scent of a dozen red roses. The flowers soothe me and I begin to feel more confident with my abilities.

The director scans the class, inviting us to examine all of the floral creations. The room is filled with a colorful array of different flowers, and I can feel the growing excitement of the students around me. "Your thoughts shape and mold the energy around you. You hold the power of creation in every thought. Now focus and practice your creative skills."

She smiles and disappears, leaving us with knowledge that will transform our very existence. We look at our flowers and begin to expand our arrangements into exotic blooms with striking colors and asymmetrical shapes.

BREAKING FREE FROM INDOCTRINATION

In a courtyard outside of the classroom, several students are discussing what we had just experienced. I stand alone and admire endless fields of flowering lavender. An impressive crystal stands like a tall sentry in the middle of the purple carpet. The sun catches the intricate peaks and valleys of the stone, shooting arcs of light across the field. The countryside reminds me of my honeymoon.

We were newlyweds sitting in a rustic cafe just outside of Paris. The espresso was hot and strong in tiny, white, ceramic cups. Just as I picture it in my thoughts, one appears in my hand. I'm amazed that the steamy liquid is just as thick and delicious as I remember. I almost expect our waiter to appear as he did when we needed directions to return to our hotel. I wonder if Tracy still thinks about me. Although I miss her and the girls, I'm beginning to feel more removed from my past life. Powerful thoughts interrupt my memories, sending me back to the classroom. As the students take their seats, the director appears.

"Most humans fail to recognize that their thoughts were never their own. Their entire way of life, including customs, social norms, and the many choices they make during their lives, is manufactured by others. Your entire reality and mindset is molded by the group thoughts of your collective. I will show you."

There's an immediate sense of motion and I'm watching myself during my past life on Earth. I see myself dressing for work and wearing my daily corporate uniform: blue pinstriped suit, red patterned power tie, white long-sleeved shirt, and polished shoes. It's strange to observe my past life now that I'm dead. I'm a classic example of complete cultural assimilation; I chased the American dream, attended my parent's church, and did everything that was expected of me. I was the prepackaged product of my surroundings. I was so busy meeting all of the expectations of others that I never stopped to question the purpose of it all. I never realized how robotic I had become.

Suddenly, there is a city street with bumper-to-bumper traffic. Taxi horns are blaring; vendors are selling newspapers on the corner as a wide-eyed man stands on a box preaching the end of the world. Busy people scurry to the confinement of their high-rise cubicles. Most are dressed the same, swinging some kind of briefcase, and all are focused on their next destination as they dodge the rising steam from the manholes. Everyone is in such a rush to get nowhere. What I don't see is anyone smiling, laughing, or appreciating any part of their day. No one is looking up at the clear, blue sky or the flowering trees that line the sidewalk. No one stops to appreciate the sweet, yeasty smell of freshly baked pastries in the coffee shop or to hear the song of the urban birds that still find places to nest in all the concrete. It looks unnervingly familiar. This was my life.

My thoughts are interrupted. "Now observe another training ground for souls."

It is as if a movie screen has appeared and covered my entire mind. But it's more real than any theater. I'm suddenly witnessing pure destruction. The images saturate my mind and drill into my heart.

Two huge armies spread along a hundred miles of trenches. Not a single tree stands. As I move closer, a valley of death and destruction fills my vision and a massive battlefield comes into focus. Men are fighting and dying and I somehow know that I'm watching the horrific Battle of the Somme during World War One. I see tens of thousands of men climbing from trenches and charging across a hellish landscape of mud and blood. Waves of young men are being slaughtered; dead and dying men hang in grotesque positions on barbed wire, like animals caught in a net. Screams of agony fill my mind. This is truly hell in its most evil incarnation. I'm stunned by the nightmare as a single question fills my mind: "Why?"

The director knows my thoughts.

"Like a newborn animal, humans bond with their immediate surroundings and all the things attached to it. They love to wrap themselves in flags and customs. It makes them feel secure to connect to the belief systems of their environment, assimilating into the temporary reality around them. Most will follow the group thought of their collective without question. In this state of consciousness they become completely attached to the labyrinth of form that surrounds them."

She pauses and observes our reaction. "As long as humans follow the dictates of the mind they will remain separated from their spiritual essence and continue to be manipulated. Souls become so deceived by the virtual reality you call Earth that they actually believe they are a physical body and a member of a tribe. They continue to repeat the same dramas and conflicts, life after life."

As I watch the battle unfold, I can feel the thoughts of the men before me. Each soldier believes he is fighting for a just cause, each feels that God is on his side. They believe they are doing their duty, and few question why.

"It takes true courage to break free from collective thought. Few humans have the inner strength to escape the grip of group consciousness. Not many have reached this point in their spiritual evolution."

My mind struggles to keep up with the director's thoughts.

"This dense reality is completely dominated by ego and illusion, so the experiences are especially challenging. The Earth school has a tough reputation; this is where soul qualities such as self-sacrifice and courage are taught."

The student next to me says, "Leave it to us to be dumb enough to go there." No one laughs.

"Earth has proven to be an effective training ground for young souls. It's brilliantly designed; no soul has ever died, and eventually, all will graduate."

Having said that, the director dissolves from view.

CHAPTER 11

CREATION TRAINING

I return to the classroom, desperately trying to comprehend what we have just experienced. At the same time I nervously wait for what is next. A mist begins to filter in through the doorway and I'm not sure what to make of this life form. It's clearly alive and moving across the floor toward the front of the room. I'm mesmerized by the movement; the body of haze swirls up to a height of about six and a half feet, stops, and becomes a human-like form. This is our new instructor—a being who appears neither male nor female. With flowing, silvery hair and shining eyes the being surveys the room. With a sound like static electricity a voice speaks to my mind.

"You may call me Remi; I'll be your instructor and guide on the next phase of your journey. I understand all of you have recently returned from the training ground you call Earth." With a nod, our new instructor says, "Nice place."

We laugh but fall silent when we see that Remi is not amused. "You will eventually return to that dense reality for further training, so my information is centered on the evolution of consciousness through the human experience."

I'm in awe of the instructor's appearance; I've never seen a being like this before and I'm captivated by its presence. I would love to know more about this soul.

"Now focus; my thoughts will flow quickly. Billions of souls remain imprisoned in the outer, dense, training realities. This class and many more are designed to assist the evolution of consciousness, especially for souls addicted to matter." Remi stops to assess our attention, and then continues.

"One of the great wonders of the universe remains a mystery for most of the earthbound humans. Every soul possesses the unlimited power of creation, but most remain unaware of their natural abilities. It's a sad irony that humans create their own reality, but fail to comprehend that they are the source of their creations. Instead of looking within for the answers, they hope and pray for some external force to save them from their own thoughts."

"So that you will better understand your own creative power, I will escort you to a dimension that borders the reality you call Earth. Now open your mind."

I feel a sense of electrical energy. The rapid transition is so jarring that I must calm my mind and adjust my focus. In this new environment I see a collection of misty, gray clouds floating around me; they vary in size, shape, and density.

The instructor directs my attention. "You are observing a physical human from a higher vibrational vantage point. Now examine the energy forms around this soul."

In front of me is the distinct image of a boy sitting on a red, beanbag chair playing a video game. He is about twelve or thirteen years old. There are band posters on the walls and clothing spread on the bed and floor. I can't help but wonder what I can learn from this boy and receive an immediate response: "Look beyond the dense physical."

As I concentrate on the space around the boy, I can see he is surrounded by an array of small grayish clouds. Some of these floating forms are highly defined while others are vaporous and lack a distinctive outer shape.

"You are observing the thought forms that are created by this soul. Notice that some of the energy forms are stable and three-dimensional while others appear as shapeless forms of mist. These clouds of energy are created by his prevailing thoughts. His dominant desires are shaping the subtle energy around him and like all developing humans, he remains unaware."

Moving closer, I examine the thought forms around the boy; three are distinctive: a skateboard, a guitar, and a cell phone. These three clouds are more structured than the other misty forms that float around him. The instructor's thoughts break my concentration.

"The more three-dimensional the thought forms become, the closer they are to manifesting in physical reality. You can see that this soul has focused his thought energy on specific creations. The well-defined forms are close to emergence into his world. Take notice, this soul remains unaware that he is creating his reality with his thoughts." Remi pauses as I examine the remarkable sight before me.

"There are more than seven-billion souls in this physical training reality and few are aware of this basic energy process. Remember, where thoughts flow, matter grows."

Around the boy are several floating forms; they are hazy and transparent. My attention is drawn to a larger energy cloud that is partially formed. As the entire class gathers around this energy I discern a shadowy outline: four wheels, two seats, and an open top.

But the other details are too vague to see clearly. I recognize that this is the outer shape of a sports car.

Remi points to the partially formed cloud. "This thought form is an energy mold in process, and as you can see it's less developed than the others. Look closely; this thought is dissipating. It lacks focus and commitment by the human, so it will not manifest in matter." Remi pauses. "You have questions?"

My curiosity gets the best of me. "How long does the energy process take to create matter?"

"This depends entirely on the focus and intensity of the directed thought energy. The more focused, the faster the manifestation. This is a universal and automatic energy process. Now clear your mind."

Instantly we move back to the classroom, I feel disoriented, but Remi doesn't miss a beat. "As you have seen, the creative power of soul is enormous, but each must awaken to their own abilities. During your next visit into matter, remember to share this knowledge with the locals."

A woman next to me asks, "Are all physical objects created by thought?"

"Yes, all matter begins as a thought and assumes shape within the inner dimensions. With repeated thought reinforcement, an energetic mold and inter-dimensional openings are developed. This process allows thought energy to manifest as form in the physical world. As humans evolve they will eventually grasp the basic energy mechanics of creation."

The instructor surveys our understanding and clarifies, "The universe can be imagined as a projection of creative light, and the physical dimension is the outermost layer of this massive hologram of energy.

Creation of form begins within the subtle spiritual core and flows outward from the source into the progressively denser vibrations of thought, emotion, and finally into matter. All form is frozen thought."

A fellow student asks, "How do we create our reality in the dense worlds like Earth?"

"First, recognize your creative power. Begin by tracing your thoughts from the first focused idea to the appearance of all the things in your life. Every object, event, and relationship in your life began as a thought. From this moment take responsibility for your creative power and consciously build your life." He pauses.

"Be aware, your thoughts are an extremely volatile power source; monitor each one with care. On a regular basis, examine your flow. Contaminated thought is destructive to the creator and toxic to all souls in close proximity, so stay clear of this poisonous energy at all costs. When you accept full responsibility for your thoughts and embrace your creative ability, all things are possible. This knowledge is now within your subconscious mind." With that, my guide disappears.

ESSENTIAL SKILLS

During my break I visit the magnificent library that is part of the training school. I sit in an overstuffed leather chair surrounded by thousands of impressive old leather-bound books. The library shelves reach higher than I can see. In silence my mind drifts as I observe the room carefully. A thick coating of dust covers each book, as though they have not been read for many years. As I examine my surroundings I realize that these books are a projection of the knowledge stored in my subconscious mind. Remi's thoughts gently bring me back to full awareness.

"As soul, you possess all the wisdom of this library and more. But, there are certain skills you must develop in order to access this knowledge. First, it's essential that you develop your inner senses so you can navigate your multidimensional self. All of this will become clear as you progress in your training."

Remi's voice grows louder in my mind and I'm drawn back to the classroom. "Know that everything is consciousness and all form is crystallized thought. For you to obtain the answers you seek you must develop your ability to focus and control your awareness."

STABILIZING AND MOVING AWARENESS

"It's important to learn how to consciously move and lock your awareness within any individual energy environment. You unknowingly did this when you entered the first nonphysical reality immediately after your death. When you embraced this construct and accepted it as your own, you became one with it. In doing so, you unconsciously locked yourself in a structured consensus-thought matrix created by a group of like-minded souls. Remember the first moments of your arrival and how quickly your assimilation occurred?"

As I review the pivotal moments of my death and rebirth in heaven, I realize that he is correct; I accepted my mother's nonphysical environment without question and assumed it must be heaven.

"To become an effective spiritual traveler, it's vital to develop your flexibility of consciousness. You must learn how to shift your state of awareness without becoming attached to the energies that dominate a given reality. We will work on this skill, but first you must learn the basics. Beyond these walls is a magnificent crystal; you have seen it before." I think back to the lavender fields outside of the training center and the impressive gemstone that stands like a gleaming beacon of light.

"Now focus on the crystal; feel that you are standing next to it. Reach out your mind and touch it. Do this now."

I clearly imagine myself standing next to the crystal, and with a rapid sense of motion I'm there. It's even more beautiful than I remember and a feeling of satisfaction flows though me as I reach out my hand and touch it. The texture is smooth and I feel an unexpected warm energy emanating from the center. The crystal's surface varies in color from the richest merlot to the most delicate lilac. As I close my eyes and open to the energy of the crystal, the warm vibrations penetrate my body. Remi appears next to me and continues his instruction.

"This is basic soul travel, lateral motion of consciousness in a structured, consensus reality. You can use the energy signature of any familiar location as your target. The key is to completely focus, know, and flow. It's essential to lock your awareness into a specific energy environment or your perception will become unstable. This skill is critical when you are attempting multiple reality jumps. Now refocus your attention back to the classroom."

I'm back standing in the classroom and feeling excited about my progress.

"Good. Now jump to the crystal and back to the classroom several times. Practice locking your awareness into each location as quickly as possible; make it automatic."

At first I'm disoriented by the rapid change of environments, but as I practice moving back and forth between the two locations I begin to feel comfortable. After several jumps I'm having fun with the speed of movement; it's exhilarating.

"All physical realities possess an energetic substructure within the outermost region of the astral dimension. Because of this you can use the memory of any physical location as a target for your jumps. Remember that distance, space, and time are meaningless. Now let's focus on another target; imagine that you are standing at the edge of the Grand Canyon in Arizona. Search your mind for the memory of this physical location; focus and know you are there."

I concentrate and feel a sense of motion and I'm instantly standing on the north rim of the canyon. The rapid change causes me to stumble backwards; I steady myself and observe the breathtaking panorama. The setting sun casts a brilliant display of orange and copper light illuminating the canyon walls. It's an incredible sight.

Remi appears and smiles. "Center yourself and lock in your awareness. Remember, consciousness has no limits. Now let's expand your ability; clear your mind and focus your complete awareness on the Earth's moon."

Following direction, I close my eyes and concentrate; in seconds there is a rush of intense motion. I find myself standing on the barren moon, looking at what appears to be a large blue marble in space. My excitement explodes as my guide appears next to me.

"During extended reality jumps, you will need to stabilize your state of consciousness. You can accomplish this by concentrating on a focusing affirmation such as: "Awareness Now!" This will help you lock your awareness into each new environment.

Practice your skills every day until your flexibility of consciousness is second nature to you. It's important to develop your nonphysical senses and your intuition. Your perception abilities are created by your mind, so you must learn to see beyond your eyes. I will show you."

I'm immediately moved to a new environment and see a magnificent stone mansion on a hill surrounded by a manicured green lawn and a high stone wall. A red Mercedes convertible pulls up to the gated entrance of the home. A beautiful woman with flowing blonde hair and a blue dress steps out of the sports car and flashes me a warm smile. I feel a wave of energy flow through me as she asks me to follow her into the house. While looking at the woman's friendly face, my thoughts are interrupted.

"Which of these things before you is an objective reality, and which are temporary thought forms created by your subconscious mind?"

I carefully examine the scene before me. The mansion's white stone columns, the sweeping stairs to the entrance, the garden statues and the neatly trimmed topiary all appear completely solid. The sunlight bouncing from the chrome wheels of the sports car is clearly real, and there is no mistaking the invitation to join this lovely woman as she waves me toward the carved mahogany doors.

I can feel the serene presence of my guide next to me. "Don't depend on your eyes; allow your inner senses to open and flow. What is real?"

After a moment of concentration, I receive a clear message. All of these things before me are thought forms created from my past physical life; a projection of my subconscious mind – nothing more than mental residue. Spontaneously I decide to do an experiment; clearing my mind, I focus on changing the color of the sports car from bright red to yellow. Within seconds the color changes to a bold yellow.

I can sense Remi's warm smile. "Yes, all of these things are your projections. Now can see how easy it is for untrained souls to become completely trapped within their own thought forms. This is a common problem for billions of souls dwelling in the physical and astral dimensions. Few souls are aware of the creative power of their own thoughts. The self-created manifestations of form make for convincing illusions in all dimensions; many humans remain imprisoned in this labyrinth of the mind."

Feeling empowered, I decide to change the color of the woman's dress from blue to red. The fabric immediately transforms into the deep red of a ripe strawberry.

"Well done. That is an effective way to test the reality of any form-based environment you experience. You can always manipulate your own thought forms; however, you will not be able to alter an established reality created by a group of souls. I'll show you."

With a rush of motion I'm standing on a hill surveying a gleaming, modern city of glass that appears reminiscent of Shanghai, China. Massive towers of translucent glass in every imaginable color fill my vision. We walk together down a busy street until we find ourselves in an older residential area. Remi stops and turns toward me.

"This is a consensus reality located within the astral dimension and inhabited by millions of souls. The collective thoughts of the local inhabitants constructed this entire city. These environments are prevalent whenever large numbers of souls direct their thoughts upon a shared concept of reality; the first heaven you experienced is one example of this energy process."

We walk down the street until I see a house that I find interesting. Directly in front of me is a weathered, wood-plank door with the Chinese symbol meaning "double happiness" carved into each side. My curiosity cannot be contained. With my newly recognized ability, I accept my guide's challenge and focus on changing the shape and color of the door. I concentrate but nothing happens.

Remi is amused by my attempt. "Consensus realities are stable energy constructs created by the collective power of many minds. This kind of energy environment is highly resistant to change. The first heaven you experienced is another example of this type of reality. From now on you will be able to determine the nature of any reality you encounter by its thought responsiveness. You will discover that consensus realities are common creations. Now rest your mind, you will need your energy for the coming lessons."

CHAPTER 12

THE POWER OF INTENTION

Standing by a wide window, I watch the sun rise over a valley carpeted with white and yellow flowers. The magnificent crystal comes to mind and I'm instantly standing in the courtyard next to the glowing guardian. While appreciating its presence, a translucent globe of light appears and glides toward me. Remi has quietly arrived. I'm fascinated by the many ways our teachers can appear to us; my thoughts are interrupted by a peaceful voice in my mind.

"The next energy principle we will explore is critical to the many souls trapped in the density of the outer dimensions." Remi's instruction shifts into a more personal mode.

"Humans are well known for weaving intricate webs of thought and then ensnaring themselves in their own creations. Our universe functions as a powerful energy mirror. With every focused thought you are broadcasting waves of creative energy into your immediate environment. Few realize that their thoughts have a powerful impact upon the subtle energies around them. I will show you this process in action."

With a sense of movement, I'm in a new environment. A young woman is sitting at a kitchen table eating breakfast with her two young children. She doesn't see or hear us. Her thoughts and emotions are being projected outward like a streaming beacon of energy, and they are transparent to me.

"My roof is leaking…I need to get it fixed. I need to get my car repaired…I can't depend on that junk in the driveway. I need to stop smoking… it's going to kill me…"

With chipped red fingernails, she jams a cigarette butt into an ashtray.

"I need a better-paying job with benefits. I don't have the money to pay my damn bills and now my kids need a dentist. I could use some luck, but what I really need is a miracle."

Remi breaks my focus, "As you can see, the thought projections of, 'need' and 'lack' saturate the space around this human. She remains unaware of her creative power and continues to focus her thought energy poorly. Through extensive trial and error this soul will eventually awaken to her abilities and begin to effectively craft a more inspired reality.

Be aware, the content and focus of your prevailing thoughts is critical to the result you experience. When you change your thoughts to, 'How can I give?' and 'How may I serve others?' a fundamental shift in energy occurs and the universe responds in kind to your thoughts. 'What can I give to you? How can I serve you?' The universe never judges or edits the content of your thoughts; it automatically responds and molds the subtle energy around you to reflect your intention. In fact, the universe has always acted on your thoughts, but it is up to you to learn how to properly manage your personal projections."

My mind struggles to process this onslaught of information. Remi senses my overload and pauses for a moment. "Remember, all form is molded by focused thought. This applies to every dimension of the universe. Souls create their own heaven or hell by the way they manage their thoughts. The spiritual teachers throughout the ages have repeatedly taught the truth of this, but few humans have listened." Remi smiles and disappears.

I feel overwhelmed and need to rest. For some reason all I can think about is the comfortable king-size bed from my past physical life; it seems like a hundred years ago. I recall the clean, crisp sheets, the foam pillow that molds to my head and the comforter that floats on top of me, giving me just the right weight to keep me warm at night. Within seconds, I'm there. I can't keep my eyes open and sink into the feather-topped mattress.

CHAPTER 13

CONFRONTING MY FEAR

After a dreamless sleep, I wake feeling refreshed. Pleasantly surprised, I find myself in a beautiful garden park; birds are singing all around me. In the distance, I hear children playing and see families having picnics on the lawn while squirrels scurry around the trees playing tag. This is so enjoyable; I would love to relax here for a while, but I know it's not to be. A stream of light appears and my training is about to continue. Remi floods my mind with thoughts.

"You have created walls around yourself with the many fears you hold. As you progress, your higher self will present you with opportunities to confront your fears. You will continue to experience this process within every dimension, including the physical. Few humans realize that every challenge in their lives is an opportunity for growth. Clear your mind; I will provide an opening."

Suddenly I'm moved to a new area of the park. Walking along a beautiful path, I'm surrounded by lush tropical flowers and pungent fruit trees. The sounds of exotic song birds echo around me. As I enjoy the colorful sights and sounds, the sky darkens and the garden quickly becomes a thick forest at dusk. Walking along this densely wooded trail, I'm surrounded by strange threatening sounds and an overpowering fear surges through me. My fear builds and I feel as though I'm being stalked by a deadly, ravenous beast. Quickening my pace, I must watch my step among the thick forest trees and knobby roots breaking through the ground. As I push through the brush I can feel that the creature behind me is coming closer. I hear raspy breath. There is a foul smell of putrid air as if it is being dragged into the mouth of a monster and pushed back out through a slash in the center of its face. In my mind, I picture the long fangs and ragged claws on the end of its gnarly paws. I sense that it can run me down and devour me whenever it chooses. My panic intensifies as any chance of escaping this beast slips away. I hear a deep growl and realize I have no weapons, no defense. Fear turns to terror as I feel the damp, warm breath of this creature on the back of my neck. I prepare myself for the worst.

Then it strikes me; I'm immortal and powerful - what am I afraid of? This is a trick of the mind. Nothing can harm me—I create my reality and nothing can stand in my way or slow my progress. At once I feel empowered and turn to challenge the creature, but instead of confronting a deadly beast I look down to see a white Persian kitten with beautiful violet eyes. I pick her up and scratch behind her ears. Caressing the soft white fur on her neck, I feel lighter, stronger, more conscious and alive.

From this moment I refuse to be limited by any manifestation of fear in my life. It's all an illusion created by my ego mind. I feel a fresh tide of freedom flowing through me as I embrace an increased sense of liberation from my fears.

Remi appears. "Confronting and then dissolving fear is a major step in your spiritual evolution. You will continue to repeat your personal lessons until your education is complete. This is a primary teaching method used for the spiritual development of soul. Now, you are ready to continue."

CHAPTER 14

THE RIVER OF THOUGHT

After the last experience I feel the need to take a break from the grueling lessons. In front of me is a beautiful grass field bordered by a wide river, and I stop on the bank long enough to gaze at the flowing water. As I do, a stone bridge takes form under my feet; I walk to the center. The river moves swiftly under me and I'm thankful for the solid thoughts that support me. My family comes to mind and I wonder how they are doing. I hope my death has not made life difficult for Tracy and the girls. I would love to see them again, and wonder how much time has passed on Earth.

I've learned much and can only imagine how deep this rabbit hole goes. But I'm at peace with myself and pleased that I've come so far. A globe of radiant light appears and I know Remi has arrived.

"The key to real inner peace is to detach yourself from the ever-changing energies around you. The mind of the evolved soul remains still, even in the center of the storm. You have grown stronger, but to experience your true self it's important to become centered in your spiritual presence beyond the mind. You must learn to free yourself from the powerful influence of group thought. The time has come to know your strength."

As instructed, I close my eyes and wait to see what challenge is next. The voice has stilled and the sound of rushing water fills my mind. I open my eyes and realize that the support of the bridge is gone and I'm standing in a raging river. The crushing power of collective human thought surges against my mind. Pounding waves of thought energy crash upon me. The river rises. Trees on the riverbank bend and break from the pressure as smaller stumps are torn away to join the onslaught. The pressure is so extreme I must focus every fiber of my being just to stand.

With growing intensity the river presses against me and I desperately struggle to hold my ground. Every facet of my mind strains against the uncontrollable current. I know I can do this. Closing my eyes, I focus deep within, calling on all my strength to fight against this terrible torrent. The pressure builds beyond all endurance and I know that I must change my approach or be swept away. I search deep within myself for a solution as Remi gently guides me.

"Allow your mind to be clear... You are completely at peace, without a ripple of thought... All energies flow through you effortlessly, for you offer no resistance... Nothing affects your peace of mind in any way... Allow all thoughts to effortlessly flow through you without resistance...

Feel yourself being transparent to all thoughts... Experience the inner peace that comes from releasing all attachments and judgments... Be the objective observer of your mind... All thoughts pass through you without resistance... You are weightless... floating free... you are the silent watcher... You are beyond the mind... Now embrace your inner self."

As I surrender to my higher self, the intense pressure immediately dissolves. I realize that I must anchor to my spiritual presence and allow this crushing flood of thought to move through me without offering any resistance. Relieved, I become transparent to the uncontrolled energies that stream around and through me. With this shift of my attention there is an immediate sense of peace and I'm free from the surging thoughts that surround me. By being transparent to all energies, I'm liberated from the relentless tyranny of thought and I can't help but smile as I watch the raging river flow effortlessly through me.

I can feel Remi's warm thoughts.

"When you become one with your spiritual essence, no power can move you. Stay anchored in your presence."

CHAPTER 15

THE CLEANSING

As I reminisce about the summers I used to enjoy at the ocean I find myself walking along a deserted beach, kicking up small explosions of sand with each step. With crashing waves in the background and the sound of seagulls overhead, I embrace the tranquil setting. This is what I loved to do in my past life; my wife and I would spend weeks at the beach, soaking in the energy of the sun. I miss those wonderful, peaceful days on the shore.

The sound of waves fade away and deep within my mind a melodic voice asks, "Are you prepared to release your attachments?"

I'm drawn back to the classroom and hear my classmates shouting.

"Yes. I'm ready."

Remi's thoughts echo in my mind. "Are you ready to release the facade?"

"Yes." Heads are nodding, and everyone appears enthusiastic as the teacher continues.

"Are you prepared to let go of everything you believe?"

"Yes!"

A blazing open furnace appears in the front of the room replacing an entire wall. The intensity of the heat is overpowering. All I can see are flames and I must cover my eyes to protect me from the searing heat.

Remi raises his voice to be heard over the roar of the fire.

"Your self-identity remains anchored in form and this obstructs your perception, slowing your progress. Consciousness has no form. You create all the obstacles you encounter and only you can remove them." He points to the flames. "Are you ready to burn away the illusions that bind you?"

I feel waves of fear emanating from my classmates as they back away from the flames. It's difficult to stand this close to the intensity of the fire.

I hear these words echo in my mind: "Now enter the flames."

My first thought is, "*Are you crazy*?" I see the fearful faces of my classmates. No one moves forward. I can feel their collective emotions; they are terrified. Time stops, my fear replaced by a driving determination that grows within. Deep down I know I'm ready for this test; mustering all my courage, I shield my face with my arms and leap into the inferno.

To my surprise, the reddish-orange flares are cool against my body. Flames swirl around me and my outer thoughts are burned away. One by one, deep-seated aspects of my ego and personality are incinerated. Layers upon layers of ingrained emotional and mental patterns fall away. Even my long-held self-identity as a male human melts away. It's a strange but liberating sensation to realize that all of my entrenched assumptions are dissolving. Clarity expands as I'm cleansed of all lingering thought and emotion. The pure white light of awareness shines through me and I can finally perceive beyond the facade of form. I feel free and sense Remi's smile.

"All form is but a temporary vehicle of soul…we exist beyond all projections of the mind. Thought is a good servant but a terrible master. Now rest, you have done well."

CHAPTER 16

THE HUMAN DREAMING FIELDS

During my break I think about my weekends sailing on the Chesapeake Bay and find myself on a thirty-foot sloop gliding silently through the water. The warm sun and breeze on my face remind me of those late spring days exploring the coves around Havre de Grace. The wind picks up and the mainsail is full. After a moment, I can no longer feel the deck, just my body floating along with the boat as it slices through the water. I feel so light and buoyant that I can barely sense my body. It's so peaceful that I would like to stay here for a while, but Remi's thoughts call me back to my training.

"Now you are ready to see the true nature of the human condition on Earth."

I'm abruptly drawn inward, far beyond my body, and float in what I can only describe as a vast void in space. Focusing my perception, I strain to comprehend the image unfolding before me. Billions of tiny lights extend outward like an endless ocean of moving, living, conscious energy. Remi knows my thoughts.

"Each light is a soul encased in a small world of projected thought energy. Each exists in self-generated reality. Few humans understand the creative life force that flows through them. Focus, I will show you the unseen energies that sustain all physical life."

I'm instantly swept into a physical-like reality and observe a sleeping man and woman; a small dog is curled at their feet. I can sense my guide next to me.

"We are just out of phase with the physical world. Closely examine the humans and their small friend."

As I stare at the sleeping couple and the dog, I notice a strange sight; they each appear as a double image and I clearly see that all three are floating just out of sync with their physical bodies. I focus, trying to comprehend what I'm observing.

"Direct your attention to the sleeping man and notice that his astral body is slightly separated from the physical body. His energy body has moved out of phase from the physical during sleep. Focus on the subtle energy connections between the two bodies of this human."

Moving closer, I watch as a trickle of liquid light flows from the floating energy body to the physical reflection lying on the bed.

"This is the essential energy-recharging process that occurs during sleep in all physical life forms. Humans remain unaware that this is the unseen purpose for sleep in all mammals. No material life could exist without it. Examine the animal; it's also charging."

Watching the sleeping dog, I witness the same energy flow and ask, "What is the purpose for this?"

"All biological life forms are powered by consciousness and cannot exist without the animating energy of spirit."

Observing the flowing energies I respond, "I'm surprised that modern science has not discovered this energy process by now,"

"Humans are so focused on matter, they see little else. Eventually they will evolve and explore beyond the density of the outer worlds. Now, direct your attention to the thought forms emanating from these sleeping souls. Look closely; examine the projections that humans call dreams."

As I focus I can see what appears to be a bubble of projected thought filling the space around the sleeping man; some of the movie-like images are fearful, while others portray intense emotional dramas of self-doubt, distrust, and selfishness. With a shift of my vision I perceive several scenes emanating from the sleeping man. The images appear like small holographic movies and I realize that I'm observing the continuing projection of this man's dream. I can see he's being chased by a group of angry, armed men and appears terrified as he runs down a narrow hallway and hides behind a door.

"Like most, he remains encased in a personal thought environment. He's working on resolving his fears and developing the qualities of soul he requires to evolve. This human, like most, remains trapped in his own repetitive thought patterns. Eventually, he will awaken from his sleep and begin to consciously explore his multidimensional self. This is a common event in the physical world, and for most earthbound souls, this is a slow and tedious process that requires lifetimes of work."

As I watch the dreams unfold I'm impressed with the creative power of the mind. I can see that this man has created a landscape of drama.

Remi instructs me to examine the sleeping woman. I watch as her ethereal astral form separates from her physical body, floats effortlessly through the window, then glides over the neighboring houses.

"Flying in a dream is common. Unfortunately she doesn't realize that this dream is actually her mind's interpretation of an out-of-body experience. She is exploring her natural spiritual abilities as her body sleeps. When she becomes more consciously aware during this experience, she will significantly enhance her spiritual growth and potential. Now, examine the dream activity of their small sleeping friend."

I shift my attention and observe the dog lying at the foot of the bed. To my surprise, I watch the dog as it runs through a green field, chasing a white rabbit. It's clearly dreaming.

"As you see, all life forms possess multiple energy bodies. The spiritual design is brilliant. Each energy body provides an effective vehicle for soul to experience every dimension of the universe. This allows all souls the opportunity to learn and evolve in many different energy environments." Remi pauses and asks, "do you observe anything else?"

Examining the sleeping man, I notice a small, dark cloud that appears to be attached to the neck of the man's floating energy body. Remi immediately knows what I've discovered and responds.

"All physical disease begins as an unseen vibrational disharmony and then slowly manifests as an outer biological disease. The energy body acts as the substructure for the physical in all life forms. This human will experience a serious personal challenge with illness in the near future. The energy disturbance will first appear in his neck. Eventually, human science will discover that all biological diseases have a subtle energy source."

As Remi examines the man's energy body he continues.

"Few humans realize that their entire lives are the direct result of energetic cause and effect. Out of ignorance they choose to believe that fate is the cause of their trials and misfortunes. Nothing could be further from the truth; every challenge is an outer reflection of your thoughts—your mind. The educational system is tough but fair; each soul creates its own curriculum for growth, and the physical world provides the three-dimensional training environment to experience the essential lessons. Look within; examine your prevailing thoughts and discover what you are creating for yourself."

CHAPTER 17

ANCHORED TO THE PAST

The sky is crystal blue and the sun gently warms my mind. Releasing all thought, I'm pulled upward as though I'm being lifted by a hot air balloon. I take a deep breath and watch the birds below me as they glide effortlessly on currents of thought. For fun, I follow their lead and imitate their flight. As I return to the ground my feet touch down gently on soft grass.

I reflect on how far I've come since the death of my physical body; I've learned about the power of thought and faced my deep-seated fears. Looking back I see that my decision to question the prevailing mindset and explore beyond my first heaven was critically important to my personal growth. A quiet voice whispers in my mind and I know class has begun.

"Only those with an open mind are ready to learn. The environments that souls experience after death are as diverse as their state of consciousness. Many humans continue to be attached to matter. Fear of change, ignorance, and their obsession with their physical identity bind them to the only environment they remember and understand. Sadly, many remain cloistered in the parallel energy dimension closest to matter, and some even attempt to interact with it. I will show you."

I find myself standing at the front of a small dilapidated house. In the dirt driveway is a large, bald man with a thick, dark beard who is attempting to start a motorcycle. It's a beautiful custom bike with midnight-blue paint and gleaming chrome wheels.

At first I assume that this man must have created his own personal heaven, but as I watch I see that he's angry and upset with his situation. Frustrated, he kicks the starter and cranks the throttle. His foot repeatedly passes through the kick-starter in a vain attempt to turn over the engine. He gets off the bike to inspect the gas tank, fuel lines, and electrical system, checking to see what is wrong. His annoyance is obvious as he desperately attempts to start the cycle again and again. I'm confused by his repetitive actions until I realize that he no longer exists in the physical world. Instead of creating a heaven for himself, he has created his own personal hell. I can't help but wonder how long he has been repeating the same actions.

"You are correct, he died years ago. Time is meaningless here. This soul is attached to his past physical life and the pleasure he received from a machine. He continues to inhabit an energy environment located close in vibration to Earth. Obsession with the past continues long after his death."

I can't help but feel sorry for him as he kicks the ground and repeats the cycle. It's clear to me that what consumes our mind will control our lives.

"There are many souls who continue to be obsessed with a physical person, an environment, or what they believe is unfinished business. Watch and see what I mean."

I feel a sense of motion and find myself in a country club standing next to a tennis court. As my vision improves, I see a dark-haired man with a grim expression and crossed arms. He is watching as a woman plays tennis with a young, fit instructor. She is all smiles as he coaches her on the proper body stance and motion of the racket. I can sense the thoughts and emotions of the glaring man. I immediately know that the man is dead and remains fixated on his past wife. An aura of jealousy and anger radiates from him as he examines her every move.

"This man died several years ago and remains obsessed with his wife's physical life. He continues to linger close to her reality so he can observe her. How can any soul progress in its evolution when it's completely anchored to the past? Many remain stuck in this limbo state of consciousness. Attachment to the past is a disease that affects both the living and the dead."

My guide pauses and adds, "This is a common block experienced by humans. Now, let's move on, I will show you more."

I'm moved to a farmhouse in the country where I observe a man and woman with three children sitting around a dining-room table eating dinner. The mom walks behind each chair and pulls spaghetti from a bowl, placing a measured amount on each plate. One of the older children is passing a bowl of sauce around in the other direction. Dad is dipping crusty Italian bread in olive oil in between sips of wine. His thoughts radiate contentment. I hear stories about how each family member spent the day. When Mom sits down to her plate, she looks at her husband with a smile as if to say, "I love our family." He winks at her.

In the corner of the room I notice a gray-haired woman watching them intently. Her hands are positioned on her wide hips and the permanent smirk she wears reveals crooked, yellowed teeth. With her stockings rolled down below her knees, I suspect she's worn this same house dress for many years. It becomes clear that she is dead and continues to be obsessed with the daily life of her son and this physical family. As I observe this woman I can inwardly feel her thoughts and can sense her past life unfolding before me. She was the mother of the man having dinner and has remained attached to her son. During her physical life she was completely focused on her only son, often interfering in his life. It's apparent that even after death her extreme attachment continues.

"Many humans remain obsessed with their past life and stay as close to the physical as possible. Their attachments bind them to the only environment they know. This woman is fixated on what she believes is unfinished business—directing her son's life. She continues to have a powerful desire to observe and even interact with the physical world. In this state of consciousness personal growth is impossible."

"Why don't you help her?" I ask.

"Change must come from within each individual. Many earth-bound souls find it difficult to let go of their past. I will show you a common situation."

CHAPTER 18

ASSISTING A TRANSITION

In the distance I see a middle-aged woman standing on the bank of a river and she appears to be calling out the name of her daughter. On the opposite river bank a girl of about twelve years old looks panic-stricken as tears stream down her cheeks. The girl strains to hear the voice of her mother from across the river and repeatedly calls out her mother's name and then waits for a response. All I can hear are faint, mumbled words that sound like prayers echoing across the water. I can clearly feel the deep desperation and loneliness of the girl as my guide speaks.

"This girl died several months ago and remains strongly attached to her earth mother. The mother's yearning to have her back in her physical life is hampering the girl's ability to progress with her spiritual evolution. She refuses to let her go and calls out to her with repeated prayers. This soul is hindered by her mother's extreme attachment because she continues to project thoughts of loss and grief instead of love. How can any soul move onward when they are held by the powerful hooks of thought?"

"Why doesn't someone help to guide the girl to a higher reality?"

"Several have tried, including her grandmother, but she continues to hear her mother's pleading thoughts and refuses to move on. She fears she will lose her mother forever if she moves out of thought range. Prolonged grieving about and attachment to the dead can become an act of self-pity. The mother would serve her daughter best by sending prayers releasing her from the past physical life and all her attachments to Earth. She could pray for the light of God's love to surround and protect her daughter from all influences that might block her spiritual progress. Any prayer or intention focused on unconditional love and spiritual release would be helpful. I will show you an effective method to assist the natural transition of consciousness that humans call death."

I close my eyes for a second to say a prayer for the young girl. In that moment I'm transported to a sparsely furnished room with stone walls. The only light comes from a number of burning candles and based on the wax drippings, I suspect that they have been burning for days. The pungent smell of incense fills the room as smoke swirls eerily around the bald heads of six Buddhist monks seated on the floor. They are dressed in simple orange robes and are gathered around a frail old man partially covered by worn blankets and lying on a humble wooden cot. It's apparent that this man is dying. There is a gentle movement of his chest with each labored breath. Watching closely, I am mesmerized by the rhythmic chanting sounds of the monks, "O brother, go to the clear light of the void! Enter the clear light!" Their commanding mantra and vibration fills the space. I watch in reverence as Remi explains in a whisper, "They are guiding this soul to go to the clear light beyond the astral dimension. They are directing him to move beyond the dense worlds of form and experience the higher reality of his spiritual essence."

I am honored to be here during this sacred moment. With a slight noise the dying man stops breathing and begins effortlessly separating from his physical body. I can see his ethereal body rise above the dull blankets and then turn toward a bright mist. He gently floats up and disappears in a flash of light. The chanting monks continue their melodic mantra as the candles radiate a pleasing glow. I don't think I've ever seen a more beautiful sight. The power of this self-less act—these monks assisting in this dying man's transition—is unforgettable.

"There is a great need for spiritual assistance in the physical world. Unfortunately, most humans remain unaware that they can assist their loved ones during this important shift of conscious-ness. Every transition is an opportunity for accelerated spiritual growth. Perhaps you can share this knowledge with the humans during your next incarnation into matter. Now rest your mind; you have much more to discover."

CHAPTER 19

CONTINUING ADDICTIONS

Seated in a white Adirondack chair on a wooden deck I have clear view to a stand of oak trees; their limbs seem to grow toward me like leafy arms. I reflect on my last experience and wonder how well I would have handled the death of one of my children. Now that I've acquired more experience, I'm sure I could offer some meaningful assistance during their transition. A breeze rustles through the green foliage, signaling my guide's arrival.

"Now you are ready to explore group-consensus environments."

I'm instantly in a new environment that pulsates with emotional energy and flashing lights. This glittering reality is a massive Las Vegas casino crowded with people focused on spinning wheels and shuffling cards. The loud sounds of slot machines echo around me. Each gaming table and roulette wheel is surrounded by people eager to place their bets. Around me is every imaginable form of gambling, including games not seen on Earth. Thousands of people are hunched over slot machines, smoking cigarettes and drinking from plastic cups.

"Many of these souls have been gambling here for decades and are completely lost in their obsessions. This is all they desire to do. As you see their ego mind control their lives." As I watch the addictions displayed before me, Remy continues.

"Humans are drawn to the group consciousness that resonates with their own. These souls remain driven by their obsessions and habits. During their past lives many were addicted to food, alcohol, drugs, gambling, or one of the many other vices that dominate the physical world. After death, their addictions continue because they are created and maintained by their mind. For many souls, these ingrained behaviors are difficult to overcome."

I must exit this reality; the stifling energies and smoke make me feel claustrophobic. After moving away from this place, I draw in a fresh breath of clean air, feeling fortunate that I didn't find this lifestyle appealing when I was alive.

"Now we will explore another human reality."

I'm moved to a new environment that appears to be the Rocky Mountains. On the very edge of a high cliff stands a group of people preparing to bungee jump. I watch in amazement as a man plummets a thousand feet down from an overhanging cliff face and then springs back with extreme speed. Screams of excitement and encouragement echo through the valley as the next jumper prepares for the great leap.

"These humans are attempting to fill the spiritual void in their lives by stimulating their senses. This is common within the outer dimensions, including Earth. They remain locked in their earthly identities, unaware that their physical-like senses are a creation of their mind. You are witnessing souls who have yet to recognize the unlimited abilities of their spiritual selves. Eventually, they will awaken and realize that they are powerful beings who can fly, transcend form, and experience the entire length and breadth of our vast spiritual universe. Now, free your mind and I will show you another group reality."

A strong tugging sensation pulls me up a steep hill. Focusing my awareness, I see that I'm standing at a high vantage point and looking down at a busy, sprawling city reminiscent of Hong Kong. Thousands of tall apartment buildings seem to climb the sides of the mountains that encircle this gleaming city of lights. The streets are overflowing with busy people going about their daily lives. My thoughts are interrupted.

"Millions of souls live in this consensus reality and continue their lives much as they did in the physical world."

Instantly I'm standing in one of the high-rise apartments and observe three people sitting at a small table. They appear to be a mother, child, and grandmother eating a humble meal of noodles. The furniture is minimal and the surroundings suggest poverty. The entire place radiates a sense of extreme boredom, and I can't help but wonder why these souls don't live in better surroundings and have a happier mindset.

"At death, souls are drawn to environments that are comfortable and familiar to them. They are attracted to the one reality they remember as solid and real; this often manifests as an energy duplicate of their past life on Earth. Most quickly conform to the collective consciousness of their peer group, just as you did when you first arrived. Like a magnet, billions of humans are attracted to the only surroundings they know and understand – matter. Sadly, their attachment to their past continues long after they die. This continuing addiction to the physical world is at the heart of the reincarnation cycle that has all of humanity in its grip."

I ask for clarification.

"At death, humans maintain their mindset; so instead of spiritual liberation, they experience a continuation of their limitations.

This is why spiritual teachers have stressed the importance of non-attachment. No external force or evil holds souls in the dense confinement of the outer worlds—humans create the walls around themselves by the very thoughts they hold dear." I nod my understanding as Remi continues.

"Each soul is drawn to the consensus reality that conforms to their state of consciousness. Generally, the new arrivals quickly adapt to the established norms inherent in the group. Most souls remain in their new surroundings because they believe they have arrived in heaven. Instead, they have unknowingly placed themselves within the confines of a highly structured, thought-created environment. You experienced this pervasive power when you entered your first heaven after your death. I will show you another group-thought reality."

After a sense of repositioning I'm standing on a busy sidewalk in an urban setting at night. I steady myself as my perception adjusts to the new surroundings. My attention is drawn to a flashing neon sign and loud music coming from a local bar. The lights beckon me to step through the swinging door. The smell of cigarettes and stale beer is overpowering. Every bar seat is filled and I feel a distinct energy of desperation and boredom mixed with self-loathing. Someone in the corner puts some coins in a jukebox and the melody of a sad country song fills the room. Men and woman in various stages of intoxication stagger around the bar. My attention is directed to a thin, middle-aged man sitting at the crowded bar. He raises a tattooed hand to get the attention of the barmaid. She refills his mug and pours him a side of whiskey. He nods and throws back the shot, chasing it with a chug of beer.

"This human has been sitting here for eight Earth years. This is what he loved to do when he had a physical body. Now, money and time are no longer obstacles to his obsessions. He eventually will leave, but only to move to another bar and pursue his addiction in a slightly different environment. And so the cycle goes.

Many of these souls will travel from bar to bar in a vain attempt to recreate their past physical life. Some have been here for decades, reliving their past and refusing to let go. The addictive-personality imprint continues long after death. Like minds are drawn together in collective realities to pursue their obsessions; humans find it difficult to escape the ingrained habits of their own minds."

As I watch the scene unfolding, a wave of sadness flows through me. The gloomy feeling of attachment permeates this entire environment. Remi redirects my attention, "I will show you one more group reality."

In the next moment, I find myself standing in the central plaza of an old European city. It takes me a few seconds to adapt to my new surroundings. Groups of men dressed in red-and-white sports uniforms are marching along a cobblestone street toward me. Cheering loudly for the victory of their home team, their booming voices break the silence of the quiet town square. They appear drunk with excitement. I can't understand their thoughts, but they are obviously supporting some kind of sports team with a wild fervor that I find strange.

As the noisy group marches by me I immediately know they are dead; however, they continue to mentally create and maintain their earthly passion. Their fanatical obsession with their favorite sports team has continued long after death. I can sense that their entire existence is now centered on their support for their team and the game they love; it's a curious sight.

"Group thought is a powerful creative force. The inhabitants remain unaware that they can be stuck in an environment fueled by their thoughts and emotions. Many of these souls have been reliving their earthly obsessions for decades of Earth time. Humans often direct their thoughts poorly; as a result they squander their most precious resource—their creative power."

Remi disappears and I'm alone with my thoughts. As I review what I've experienced, my mind is in overdrive. At first, I didn't wish to believe my observations because this knowledge conflicts with my childhood religious teachings. I was told that at death we enter the ultimate reality called heaven. Now I see that for many of us a utopian spiritual world is but a dream. It's now clear that most people will experience an energy environment similar to their physical existence. Millions will continue to repeat the same behaviors and attach themselves to group realities that are comfortable to them. It's a strange situation; we who possess the ultimate power of creation use our abilities to recreate mundane realities from our past.

But to be fair about it, I realize that I was no different; my first heaven was a pleasant duplicate of my earthly environment and was dominated by the group's beliefs. I also see that it's up to me to change my thoughts, for when I altered my state of consciousness, my external reality also changed.

CHAPTER 20

INDIVIDUAL ATTACHMENTS

After considering my last lesson I can't help but wonder how long I've been repeating the same actions? What attachments do I hold that are slowing my personal spiritual growth? As I meander through the lovely garden of the training school, Remi appears next to me and responds to my thought.

"You will learn the answer to this soon; have patience. Now I will show you another human reality; this one is created by the mind of only a single soul."

Instantly I'm standing outside of a small, ranch-style home in what feels like a typical suburban neighborhood. It feels inviting, so I walk past the oversized mailbox and up to the front porch, where several boxes have been delivered and await collection by the owner. My guide and I enter the home but are immediately blocked by large mounds of junk that fill the living room. Walking through the home is difficult. The floor is completely covered by piles of magazines, books, pictures, small kitchen appliances, and an extensive collection of painted plates and small figurines. Boxes of jewelry, cosmetics, and shoes are stacked to the ceiling, while racks of clothes and handbags cover every wall. In the corner, a middle-aged woman sits alone in a faded green recliner.

Her head is cocked to one side to keep a cordless phone in place between her ear and shoulder as she pages through a catalog with colorful display ads. In the background, I hear a television ad blaring, *"But that's not all; if you order in the next five minutes, we'll double your order. That's right..."*

"This soul is obsessed with meaningless objects and she believes that these things are essential to her existence. Unfortunately, this is a common issue in the physical and astral dimensions. She died long ago and has existed here for decades in Earth time. Like many humans she is so attached to her past physical life and her possessions that her mind has created an energy replica of her last earthly environment. She finds comfort in this familiar reality and is convinced that she has found heaven."

As I examine my strange surroundings, I think, *this is crazy. I must be extremely careful how I focus my attention.*

"After death, many humans are shocked by the dramatic change of their existence and subconsciously create a duplicate energy reality where they can feel comfortable and secure. As you see, spiritual stagnation can be the result."

"Why don't you help her?"

"Go ahead and try." Remi smiles and waves his arm in her direction.

I carefully step around the piles of junk and approach the woman warmly. "Hi, my name is Frank. And you are?" She doesn't answer or take my extended hand. This is awkward, but I continue attempting to communicate with her.

"You don't have to remain here; there's an entire universe to experience and enjoy."

She ignores me, so I try again. "You can go anywhere and create anything you desire."

She barely whispers a response. "This is what I want."

I pick up a catalog and wave it around the room, pointing to the insanity of the surroundings. "But all of this is meaningless junk."

She jumps up and screams, "Don't touch my stuff! Put it back."

I feel waves of anger as she scowls. I toss the catalog back on one of the heaps of debris and she appears to settle down. "Leave my stuff alone. Get your own." Like a child, she grabs a woven blanket on the arm of her recliner with one hand and a stuffed toy dog with the other. "Get out of my house!"

With the thought of exiting I'm quickly out of the house, and question whether the stuffed dog was a representation of a past physical pet.

"Yes, even the toy dog is a thought projection from her past life. Most humans accept only three-dimensional objects as real. Their attachments continue to dominate their state of consciousness and their reality. "

MISGUIDED COMFORT

"Now, follow my thoughts; we will visit another self-created reality."

My perception shifts and I'm standing in what appears to be a modern kitchen observing an obese woman who looks to be about twenty-five years old. Her stringy red hair is held away from her plump face by an elastic headband. Sitting at a small table devouring a large tray of chocolate brownies, she occasionally licks her chewed-down nails at the end of her chubby fingers.

Two wall ovens and a large double-door refrigerator dominate the space around her. She is so focused on consuming her treats that she doesn't see me enter the room. As I glance at the open pantry, I see a wide selection of food in cans, boxes, bags and jars. On the shelves are cookbooks and canisters filled with various spices and mixes. The countertop extends for several yards and is covered with an assortment of appliances: a mixer, a sandwich maker, a food processor, and other devices that I don't recognize. She stares into space as she consumes her brownies, looking up only to shift her attention to a large cream pie sitting on the counter.

"This soul is reliving the joys of food she remembers from her physical life. She was unhappy during her past incarnation but always found pleasure in cooking and eating her creations. Food was her comfort and the one thing she could count on. As you can see, she is completely addicted to this pleasure."

As I watch this woman I think to myself, *if we only had the knowledge and discipline to focus our thought energy wisely, the entire human species would be transformed overnight.*

Remi responds to my thoughts. "True, but the real question is; how do you effectively achieve this?"

I contemplate the awesome nature of this vast multidimensional educational system of which we are all a part. I used to think that Earth was the only training ground of soul but now I know the truth; the challenges and lessons continue far beyond the body. Now I see that each of us create our own lessons and the time our training may take is meaningless. A deep feeling of compassion for all souls flows through me; life after death can be just as demanding as the physical world. As this realization sinks in, my instructor leaves me to my thoughts.

CHAPTER 21

HELLS OF THE MIND

Back in the classroom, I'm alone to reflect. My instruction has grown more intense and I realize how little I know about myself and my existence. I hear Remi's voice echo in my mind and I know that my lessons are continuing.

"Many humans remain obsessed with the existence of hell. Their concepts are often primitive and heavily influenced by their religions. The entire concept of eternal hell and punishment was created by humans for the purpose of manipulation and control. Focus, and I will show you the reality of hell."

I find myself standing in the center square of a small town. Remi appears and directs me to a dark-haired woman sitting on a bench. She appears to be around twenty years old and is tenderly holding a baby in her arms. As I approach the woman I feel the need to see her child. Because the child is wrapped in a blanket, it's difficult to observe its face, so I step close and pleasantly ask, "Hi, may I see your baby?"

She smiles and opens the top of the blanket. I can't believe my eyes. Before me is the outer shape and form of a baby but there is no human face; instead, there's only a lump of clay-like material. I look again at the mother's face, which is clear in every detail; I can see her blue eyes and the freckles on her nose, so I know my perception is accurate. I examine the baby again and see what appears to be a lifeless lump of grayish clay with no discernible face.

My thoughts run wild. *My God, this is not a baby!* But I don't wish to alarm the woman. Attempting to be diplomatic, I gently say, "You have an unusual baby."

With a beaming smile, she responds, "Yes, isn't she beautiful?"

Unsure of how to respond, I ask, "Who does your child look like?"

The woman glares at me like I'm crazy. "She looks just like me, silly."

I'm confused and respond, "Can I help you in some way?"

"No, my baby and I are fine." She reacts defensively, pulling the blanket back around the baby as if to protect her from me.

I try my best to offer some assistance. "If you ask for help, you will receive it."

"We don't need anything. Get away from us." Her tone is angry and she turns away.

"Maybe I can have someone assist you. There are guides available who can help you through this."

"I don't need anybody! Get away!" she shrieks and I feel waves of her anger roll over me.

Suddenly, it feels like a powerful vacuum is drawing me back to the classroom. Upon returning, my first reaction is, "What was that? That thing was not a baby, what was it?"

A flash of insight flows through me. *She was holding a thought form of her dead baby. This woman and her baby died together in a car crash long ago in the physical world. She continues to feel responsible and remains attached to her dead child and her role as a mother. She can't let go. I sense the baby has transitioned to a new reality, but the mother has remained in complete denial of her death. She created an energy form of her baby with her thoughts. In her mind, the baby is very real in every respect; she perceives a beautiful baby face and even hears the baby breathing. I didn't see the face of the baby because I don't accept her personal projection of reality. I realize that the woman continues to feel intense guilt over the death of the child and refuses to accept the traumatic change that instantly occurred at the moment of their death together.*

Remi knows my thoughts.

"Very good, you are opening to your inner senses. This soul is a prisoner of her guilt and has created her own personal hell. Some humans continue to hold negative thoughts and emotions after their death; by doing so they create their own hells of the mind. In their shame and self-loathing, they experience the result of their own energy projections. Hell is not a place—it's a state of consciousness."

I feel sorry for this woman and disappointed with myself for not being able to help her. I've witnessed many strange behaviors in heaven and I now realize that they are the result of human obsessions, guilt, fear, and addictions. For some people, the shock of their death is more than they can accept. I can only imagine the intense suffering this mother must have endured; one moment she was happily living her daily physical life with her child, and the next instant she was thrust into a radically different reality.

Remi adds, "This kind of distress often occurs when there is a sudden or violent death. Some humans refuse assistance after death; this soul will linger in this state of consciousness until she is ready to change."

"Why can't someone like you help her?"

"Several have tried. All souls possess free will to believe and create what they like; and all shifts of consciousness are an internal process."

I nod in agreement but don't comprehend why she can't be helped.

"Soon you will understand, but now I will show you another self-created reality."

I'm immediately moved to a gray melancholy setting; heavy, dark emotions fill the space. Sitting on a rock outcrop is a young man; he appears troubled and lost in his thoughts, his face emotionless and withdrawn. I feel the need to move closer and ask, "Are you all right?" He doesn't acknowledge my presence and appears to be in a deep depression. I open my mind and allow the impressions to flow.

I see this man's past physical life unfold before me; rapid pictures flowing through my consciousness. In his mind, the past drama is happening now. He's a young soldier reliving the chaos of house-to-house fighting in Baghdad, Iraq. His platoon is taking fire from the second story of a house. Next to him, a close buddy is shot in the stomach and falls to the ground in agony. After several critical moments, he throws a grenade through a window. Upon entering the house he's traumatized to see that along with the Iraqi soldier, the explosion killed an entire family, including two young children. I can sense his dark emotions as he clings to his self-generated guilt and refuses to forgive himself.

"Sadly, this soul has manifested a personal hell. No external force has created this situation. Eventually he will forgive himself and move to a higher vibrational reality. Time is meaningless, so hells of the mind can last for hundreds of Earth years. It's unfortunate that so many humans continue to overlook the critical importance of self-forgiveness." Remi pauses for a moment to see if I understand." To give you a greater perception of the wide diversity of these realities, I will show you another self-created hell."

I'm standing inside an urban loft apartment with large windows and a wide wall of floor-to-ceiling mirrors. I see a young woman standing in front of the mirrors, brushing her styled, platinum-blond hair. She leans in to her reflection inspecting her skin, assuring herself that her makeup is as perfect as it can be. Looking satisfied, she puckers her ruby-red lips and blows herself a kiss. Smoothing down the sides of her skin-tight mini-skirt, she turns to the right and left a half-dozen times. I see her nodding her head with approval. A living Barbie doll, she is obsessed with making sure that every hair and curve is molded to her personal image of perfection. She crosses the room and throws open a double-door closet revealing hundreds of shoes.

"This human has created a thought projection of her astral body. This is the appearance she attempted to achieve while in the physical world. She has existed here for decades of Earth time, preening her current energy body into her own twisted vision of beauty. Her self-identity and state of consciousness are completely focused upon her dense human form. She sees and knows nothing else. Sadly, this kind of self-generated reality is common; this soul has confined itself to a tiny segment of the astral dimension with other souls of like mind. After death, many humans remain attached to their physical self-image and unaware that their body is but a fleeting vehicle of consciousness—a construct of their mind."

Remi pauses and shakes his head. "How can any soul evolve beyond its own dense self-conception? There are billions of humans currently existing in the self-created realities of their minds. The most insidious hell is the one that you create."

I stare in disbelief and realize that as much as I would like to help, the resolution to this insane obsession can come only from within this woman. The human mind can create deceptions beyond anything I ever imagined possible.

"I will show you one more self-generated reality."

The environment shifts and I see a middle-aged man with a paunchy belly in a white tank top. He sits alone in a large brown recliner, watching a sports channel. The volume of the baseball game is extremely loud. In one hand he holds the remote control and in the other a can of beer. His surrounding reality is a dark void in space containing only two solid structures—the television and the chair. As a commercial starts, he immediately changes the channel from baseball to football. The environment is so strange I struggle to comprehend the nature of this reality. Remi senses my confusion.

"This human has intentionally cloistered himself from other souls. His physical life was difficult and filled with personal disappointment. He feels that his entire family and everyone he knew abandoned him during his past life; he died holding a deep resentment toward all people. He distrusts everyone and refuses to allow anyone in his personal space. He focuses on the only source of pleasure he can remember: his TV shows and the comfort of his chair."

The blaring sound of the television fades as I observe the bizarre sight before me. It's clear that the afterlife is far more complicated than I ever imagined possible. Our thoughts are a powerful double-edged sword that shapes our reality now and after death, and as a result, we create both heaven and hell for ourselves. I realize more than ever that I must be extremely careful how I focus my thoughts and intentions.

My teacher adds a final thought and then fades from view.

"Spiritual stagnation is the real hell. As long as souls believe they are a human body, they will continue to imprison themselves in the outer dimensions of the universe."

CHAPTER 22

CREATION IS ART

Waiting for my teacher I collect my thoughts. As my lessons continue I realize the importance of an open, flexible mind, and I'm curious about what may be next. Remi appears as a sphere of light and I'm absorbed in his presence.

"As you have seen, all form-based realities are molded by thought. A wide spectrum of magnificent worlds flowing with endless levels of love and light is available to you. I will show you one of many environments existing in the higher vibrational regions of the astral dimension."

With a shift of perception, I find myself in a beautiful botanical garden. A peaceful, loving energy radiates from every tree and blade of grass. I'm surrounded by lush, bright-green lawns and a wide assortment of colorful flowers. Radiant blue ponds reflect a multitude of brilliant colors from the exquisite hanging flowers that border them. This reminds me of the magnificent fairways I enjoyed when visiting the Augusta National Golf Club in Georgia. As I stroll along the winding paths, I see groups enjoying picnics and taking walks.

"Creation is taught on many different vibrational levels and can manifest in a wide variety of art forms." Remi explains.

As I appreciate the breathtaking vistas, I watch several artists standing near large, floating easels made of light. They are creating vibrant landscapes with the power of their minds. Each creation comes alive with color and glows with life. There are several art forms I have never seen on Earth, including floating, three-dimensional holograms of light that change color and density according to the thoughts of the artist. I witness a kaleidoscope of flowing colors and shapes. An intricate projection of moving, living light creates a stunning display that is glorious to behold. The brilliant visual complexity of each creation appears to extend into infinity.

"Here you will find many souls who are exploring their unlimited artistic talents. Creation itself is art." Remi's gentle-toned voice fills my mind.

Captivated by the beauty that surrounds me I ask Remi for some time alone.

"I would like to explore this reality."

"Take as long as you need. I'll be waiting when you are ready to move on. "

In the distance I see a hill covered in yellow daffodils; a young woman with shining red hair stands out in contrast, her white dress flowing casually in the breeze. I watch as she creates detailed landscapes from the clouds floating high above me. As the clouds float closer I realize that they are not clouds at all, but massive white thought forms being shaped and molded by the focused intention of this artist. I'm impressed by the skill of this talented soul. Magnificent white-capped mountains and spectacular multicolored waterfalls fill the sky. This floating three-dimensional artwork extends as far as I can see. The entire heaven is her canvas. I consider the incredible potential of these grand creations and wonder if this is how new realities are formed in the denser dimensions.

I'm drawn to explore this beautiful place where even more diverse expressions of artistic craftsmanship are exhibited. There are soft, flowing energies, intricate patterns of light, brightly painted scenes on living canvas, and sculptures of birds that appear to be mid-flight; each creation is lovelier than the last. Every soul appears vibrantly alive and overflowing with brilliant energy. Soothing melodies from a flute accompany a dancer so fluid that I think she may drift into the air. As I watch her effortless movements I realize that her feet are not touching the ground at all. As I look to my left, a poet paints flowing three-dimensional verses in the air with his index finger extended like a pen. As the prose is displayed, he reads the lines with a gentle voice.

There is a picturesque cottage nearby, so I go there to soak in the creative energy all around me. I manifest a hammock in the corner of a screened porch overlooking a cool mountain lake that has been created in soft watercolors. Tall pines sculptured from thought surround me. As I lie comfortably in the folds of the swinging bed, I relax and close my eyes. Exhausted, I sink into sleep but immediately feel a powerful vibration surging through me. I let go and flow with it. There is concentrated motion, then stillness; I release all thoughts and embrace a new kind of experience.

I melt into an existence without shape or form. There are no directions or reference points and it feels as though I'm floating in an ocean of unconditional love. I surrender and enjoy the freedom, the pure bliss of being. It's beyond my wildest dream.

As I float, I'm transformed into a flowing stream of musical notes, my unique sound extending beyond all thoughts and form. With an explosion of joy my awareness expands as a soaring creation of pure, endless music. There are no constraints, for each note is an expression of me. I am the sound existing through all time and space, throughout all forms of life and through every dimension of creation. I am part of everything. My song fills the universe, and I realize it was only my own obsession with the one note of form that held me in the lower worlds. We are so much more than I ever imagined possible. I can create anything I choose to accelerate my evolution, for all form is but a frequency.

Gently returning to my body, I pause to take in the glorious sights and energies that flow around me. I feel lighter, completely refreshed. This is more like my ideal concept of heaven than any place that I have experienced so far. I would love to spend more time among these talented souls; maybe this could be a future home for me. But for now I know I have much more to learn.

CHAPTER 23

RELIGIOUS TERRITORIES

After my exploration of the artist world I feel refreshed and ready to continue my training. Remi greets me with a warm smile.

"Now you have seen how the human afterlife is created by collective states of consciousness. I will show you the pervasive power of group thought."

At my feet there is a worn, stone path. I'm surrounded by structures that appear to be thousands of years old; some are crumbling, some intact, but all are lacking any modern features. Men in cloth robes and wide leather belts are rushing along a cobble stone street. This is a sprawling and crowded ancient city. The rhythmic call for prayer echoes through the alley. The haunting sound floods my mind as an endless stream of people move along the busy streets, heading toward the glimmering golden mosque in the center of town. Two minarets reach to the clouds guarding the massive structure. The gold dome of the mosque glows like a burning flame in the sky. It's an impressive sight. The men wear long robes and the women follow behind them in black garments. Thousands file through the narrow streets streaming toward the mosque. I feel drawn to follow a group of worshipers and notice that all the men have beards while the women are covered from head to toe in flowing, dark robes. I pause for a moment and watch the lines of the faithful entering the mosque.

My guide speaks. "It's common for humans to continue their beliefs after death. Because of this, every religion on Earth, both past and present, is reflected in the afterlife. Each faith creates their own consensus reality firmly molded by the group thought of the local inhabitants."

"How many religious heavens exist?"

"More than any soul can count. Each is created by the group consciousness and they are always expanding in number and complexity. As you discovered when you entered your first heaven, most souls will accept the first environment they experience after their death; they know no better. Now clear your mind; I will show you another."

I hear church bells and find myself standing within the upper deck of a massive, cathedral-type structure and surrounded by a large gathering of souls. This is by far the largest and most magnificent church I've ever witnessed. The walls and ceiling appear to be made of translucent blocks of glowing light. Massive, arched, stained-glass windows fill the structure with ethereal streams of color and light. Ten thousand souls sing a religious hymn as the entire building vibrates with the power of their song. Waves of emotion sweep through me; I'm overwhelmed by the energy and passion of the gathering.

As the hymn fades, a charismatic religious leader draped in gleaming white robes seems to magically appear at the pulpit and begins an impassioned sermon to this huge congregation of the faithful. His booming voice captivates the throng of followers. They hang on his every word.

"Our Lord Jesus has blessed us with the gift of everlasting life and we patiently await his return. Rejoice; we are the chosen of the Lord and are born again in spirit. Rejoice; we are the children of the Lord and dwell in the Promised Land. Be steadfast in your faith, for the return of our beloved savior is at hand."

My mind reels with a numbing realization: millions of souls are still waiting for their savior to appear. I had always thought that at death people would be spiritually reunited with God in heaven. At the very least, I thought they would be enlightened by the dramatic change they experience during death. I thought that all people would awaken to the reality of their immortality and this would accelerate their desire for personal spiritual development. But now I see the bitter truth—millions continue as before.

Remi knows my thoughts.

"These souls believe they have been saved from the torments of some biblical hell and have entered the ultimate heavenly paradise. They believe this pleasant simulation of an Earth-like reality is the promised heaven of their religious faith."

I watch the spectacle unfold as the entire congregation is moved to tears by the intense energy that fills this gleaming cathedral. The skilled presentation of this charismatic religious leader is impressive. This man is a master at creating, arranging, and projecting powerful waves of intense emotional energy. The entire congregation is locked on to his every word. I can feel his powerful thoughts wash over me, and like a master musical conductor he directs the audience with hypnotic authority.

Grasping a glowing, white Bible in his hand, he declares, "We are the chosen, the children of God. Follow the sacred word and rejoice in your salvation. Rejoice; the return of our Lord is at hand…"

The preacher gives a polished and stirring performance as he leads the large gathering with high-energy music and song, telling them what they desperately wish to believe. A roar of applause emanates from the massive congregation as he announces the church's expansion.

I'm surprised; even death provides no escape from the beliefs we carry with us. Since Jesus didn't appear when these people died, the religious leaders created a revised doctrine to keep believers engaged in the faith. Despite being dead, the devoted are still waiting for their savior to appear.

Remi senses my distress. "For many, the idea of change is threatening and the comfort of the familiar is welcomed. These souls, like all inhabitants of the astral dimension, are precisely where they need to be at this point in their spiritual evolution. The length of time this process may take is meaningless."

Now I understand why so many souls are drawn to these attractive environments after death: it's far easier to be a religious follower than a spiritual explorer. Exactly how many of these realities exist is unknown, but I'm sure all of them have one thing in common: they are gilded cages created by the shared thoughts of the inhabitants. Believers remain content in their pleasant religious communities: it's alarming to think how many of these souls have limited themselves to the confines of the astral dimension. The exposed truth of our afterlife is far more shocking than any work of fiction.

My guide responds to my thoughts. "Humans often confuse a moving emotional experience with a spiritual awakening. Most possess no reference point and are often moved by the power of group emotional energies. Reflect on how this knowledge affects you. When you are ready you will experience the next consensus reality without me."

THE POWER OF CONSENSUS THOUGHT

The numbing reality of my last session lingers as I close my eyes and fall into a dreamless sleep. With no objects around me, I simply drift. After a few moments, I sense I'm being drawn to a new location. I can't control it, so I release and go with the flow. Above me, I see an azure sky with dozens of fluffy cloud formations and I realize that I'm lying on my back. I feel the cool grass gently touching the back of my neck and arms as I watch the white clouds drift lazily by.

Interested to know more about where I am, I sit up and look around. It's a bit unsettling to see that I'm in the middle of a cemetery, surrounded by headstones. As I turn my head to the left, I see a stone monument etched with my name and the years of my physical birth and death. Inscribed are the words "Devoted Husband and Loving Father." I turn to my right and see the headstone for my mother; it reads "Loving Mother and Loyal Friend." For the first time since I departed from my first heaven, I think about my mother and wonder what she is doing. Now that I've explored other existences and know more about the nature of heaven, I could go back and share what I've learned.

Feeling familiar vibrations, I surrender to a powerful tugging force drawing me in. I feel disoriented, so I command myself to focus. After a moment, my clarity improves.

I'm standing alone on the sidewalk in front of my mother's house and realize that I've returned to my first heaven. My old home is quiet and strangely devoid of life. Before me are the familiar rows of small homes with white picket fences and I expect to see my mother in the front garden tending her flowers. In the near distance I hear the faint sound of singing and music emanating from the small white church I used to attend. When I think of walking to the church I'm instantly standing at the front steps.

The welcome sound of organ music greets me as I float effortlessly through the tall, double doors. Spontaneously, I float to the back of the church and hover near the ceiling by the choir loft as I observe the church service. The congregation of about a hundred people are singing a familiar psalm as the pastor stands at a raised white pulpit and appears to direct the music. I remember him well; this is the same man who orchestrated my religious intervention. Scanning the congregation I see my Aunt Sophie sitting next to my mother in the third row and I slowly float toward them. Suddenly, the pastor stops singing and glares up at me. He appears stunned and then terrified. To my surprise he explodes in anger as he points at me, screaming, "Be gone! Leave this house of the Lord. You don't belong here."

The singing abruptly stops, and the entire congregation turns to stare at me. My mother begins to stand, but is quickly pulled back into her seat by my aunt. The pastor shouts again, "You don't belong here. Be gone!" Mass hysteria ensues and I can feel the heavy, fearful thoughts of those assembled. I'm bewildered by their extreme negative reaction; *I used to live here, they should recognize me.* Instinctively I float higher and drift above the frightened congregation while watching the growing chaos below me. *I would love to show them what I've learned. Why are they so hostile?* Their fear turns to jabs of anger as their thoughts ring out.

"He can fly; it's witchcraft."

"It's the heretic; Lord deliver us."

Waves of intense emotional energy hammer me, and I know it's time to leave. Floating up to the highest peak of the ceiling I look down at my mother as I exit through the church roof and fly from the insanity below. Immediately I feel relieved and soar up and away at extreme speed.

Upon returning, I take some time to relax and review the meaning of this intense experience. I now realize that the heaven I first experienced is but one of millions of consensus realities. I've learned from personal experience that souls enter and embrace comfortable environments that are centered upon their state of consciousness and beliefs. Those of like mind are drawn together because of their shared thoughts and beliefs. Group consciousness is what shapes and molds the countless realities that form the various heavens.

Now I understand that assimilating into any single group-consensus reality can potentially slow our individual spiritual growth. The local inhabitants of my first heaven created serious collective limitations; they could not fly, move through walls or even answer the basic questions of their existence. The beauty and comfort of my first heavenly reality disguised the extensive limits created by the group consciousness of the souls living there. And I also see that we carry our ingrained physical indoctrination and our dense self-concept with us when we die. What hinders our personal spiritual growth in the physical world can and will continue to do so in the afterlife; now more than ever I see the importance of questioning everything. I also know that I'm forever changed and I can't go back to being the old me; I release the past and take joy in my continuing journey.

CHAPTER 24

HEALING ENVIRONMENTS

My training has stretched my mind beyond what I believed was possible, and my vision of the afterlife will never be the same. Soon I will continue my lessons and there is little time for relaxation. A soft light appears and shakes me from my drifting state of consciousness. With some effort I focus and prepare for my next lesson. Remi's thoughts gently enter my mind.

"During each day on Earth, more than a half-million humans exit their current physical bodies. Many souls entering the nonphysical realities have incurred serious emotional and psychological damage that remains lodged in their subconscious minds. Their energy bodies reflect the suffering and deterioration that they experienced while visiting the physical world. Many humans require extensive energy adjustment and clearing. The energetic blocks of hate, fear, and anger must be cleansed before a soul can continue its journey of awakening."

My awareness is directed to a massive hospital complex.

"There are many healing environments designed for the benefit of souls entering the nonphysical realms. Millions of loving and talented individuals devote their entire lives to the service of newly arriving souls; they provide the essential care and nurturing needed for recovery from the earthly ordeal. They are a true inspiration."

I'm transported into a long hallway where I view groups of doctors and nurses in white uniforms moving quietly from room to room. They look busy but relaxed. Several small groups of medical personnel appear to be consulting over the diagnoses and treatments of various people. Walking through the halls, I see that many of the patients appear to be sleeping or in a coma.

Remi leads me to a large, softly lit room with a row of white beds occupied by people who appear to be asleep.

"These newly arriving souls are receiving energy restoration and dream therapy. They have experienced serious trauma during their physical life and are being healed in the dream state. This is one of many healing centers designed to assist new arrivals from Earth. Large numbers of generous beings devote their entire existence to the healing of returning souls after their deaths. Emotional cleansing, energy-body renewal, and form-addiction counseling are just a few of the therapies offered here. A wide variety of healing centers are specially designed for the rehabilitation of souls who are adjusting to the transition of death."

Remi directs my attention to a window.

"This is an enormous endeavor. Many arriving souls require prolonged assistance and loving care in order to adapt to their new lives beyond their physical bodies. The power of love combined with the serene vibrations of nature provides a potent restorative force. The healing energies of light and sound infused with unconditional love help to heal the energy bodies of all new arrivals. As each soul's energy body is restored, it can better adapt to its new life. However, even with the large number of spiritual helpers and healers available to assist in their transition, arriving souls must be open to accepting assistance."

I'm directed to another room and see a woman floating several inches above a bed and surrounded by hundreds of soft white light filaments. The room is filled with an unusual but pleasant humming vibration.

"This soul's subtle body is being energetically adjusted and cleansed with healing light and vibrational energy. Most humans mistakenly believe that they experience their soul after death; but most simply shift their awareness to their inner energy body. I will show you another healing space."

I'm moved to the interior of another environment; this room is a pure-white cube about twenty feet in diameter with soft, segmented walls. The entire interior is covered in deeply etched glyphs reminiscent of an ancient Egyptian language. Upon entering, my entire body and mind are saturated with high-frequency waves of energy that are difficult to describe. A man floats in the center of the room and appears to be in a coma or deep asleep.

"This soul's physical body died from cancer and his subtle body reflects the debilitating effects of the disease. The healing frequencies of this space are aligning and rebalancing the energetic matrix of this soul's astral body until it's fully restored. Many arriving humans require this form of energetic healing assistance."

I'm amazed at the amount and quality of assistance that is available to us. The sheer magnitude of this facility is impressive, and I'm told that this is but one of thousands. Calling this a building is an understatement; it's more like an enormous site filled with every imaginable thought-created environment—lakes, rivers, forests, and oceans—all used for therapy and healing. Some of these areas look familiar to me. The entire surroundings radiate calm, healing energy that frees my mind. I'm drawn to explore the beautiful grounds. I select a path along a stream and feel the need to follow it.

WELCOME AND ORIENTATION CENTERS

I stop along the way to appreciate gray squirrels zipping around the trees and the chipmunks scooting from one little hole in the ground to another. Lingering on a small bridge over a pond, I'm amused to see a beaver poke his head up through the reeds and then continue on his quest for more building materials. Crossing the path in front of me is a deer, quickly followed by her fawn. I can see why a beautiful environment like this would soften a traumatic transition. My travel resumes until I reach a clearing; it appears as a wide, green field next to an ancient, stone castle. Remi appears next to me and continues the lesson.

"All souls are met at the transition you call death and escorted to an appropriate place for their state of consciousness. This is normally done by loved ones of the new arrival."

"Yes, I remember well. My mother met me."

"During times of mass human upheaval, such as wars and plague, millions of loving souls assist the new arrivals to adapt to their existence beyond the physical. If a loved one is not available, volunteers are on call to assist the arriving souls. Focus and I will show you."

In front of me is the aftermath of a horrific battle from the American Civil War. Thousands of men dressed in blue and gray are wandering through a green field; they appear completely lost and bewildered. I can see that most of the men look to be in shock as they stagger aimlessly and call out the names of their fallen brothers. The environment feels chaotic due to the racing thoughts and intense emotions of so many confused and lost souls. Some of the men are joyfully met and embraced by loved ones, while others are approached by helpers who provide comfort and answers to their questions. Slowly, the dazed souls try to absorb the stark reality of their death. Walking together to the edge of the green field, their bodies seem to disappear in a white mist.

Remi fades from view and I'm drawn to see more on my own. I think of the soft energies of the healing center and find myself sitting in a quiet chapel among several people in deep meditation. There is an ethereal rainbow of velvety light streaming through the tall, stained-glass windows. The colors fill the room and bathe me in a peaceful glow, warming my very soul. This is a special place where all are welcome. With a deep sense of tranquility and unconditional love, I close my eyes and soak in the flowing energies that fill this space.

It's such a peaceful feeling that I don't want to leave. Relaxing, I breathe in the vibrations moving through me. The warm energies heal my mind, like they have for so many before me.

CHAPTER 25

NONHUMAN HEAVENS

The beauty and peace of the chapel are etched in my mind and I feel recharged and ready for my next adventure. As if reading my thoughts, a beam of golden mist appears and I know that Remi has arrived.

"There are many training grounds created for the education of soul—more than anyone can count. Humans play but a tiny part in the many schools of form. To show this diversity, I will introduce you to two different nonhuman realities."

My guide's thoughts propel me to a new environment. I'm unprepared for the intense colors and unusual shapes and have never seen anything like it before. What appears to be an ocean of flowing mercury is bordered by a vast forest of giant, red mushrooms as tall as redwoods. Drawn to a rocky waterfront, I watch as the crashing ocean waves change color from bright silver to dark amber. In the distance there is a strange creature on a large outcrop of rocks; it appears to be a large, gray slug. It's about six feet in length and has several eyes set in horizontal rows. Its mouth, nose, and ears look like the gills of a fish. As I take in the amazing sight before me, I realize that this alien being is manipulating the color and shape of the ocean waves with the power of its mind.

"You are correct; this soul is learning to control and focus its creative thought energy. Just like you, its body is molded by its self-conception.

Even its spiritual training is similar to yours—evolution through the use of form. You have much in common."

I stare in awe as the alien changes the colors of the pounding waves. I'm fascinated by the immense skill of this soul as it manipulates its environment and controls an entire ocean with its thoughts. This soul is obviously far more advanced than I.

"You possess the same abilities. Soul has no limits."

I wonder about the life of this being, and question if it's somehow connected to me and to all humanity.

"All souls are connected; the outer shape and appearance of the body are unimportant, for all energy bodies are but temporary vehicles…your evolution with all consciousness is intertwined."

I look to Remi for confirmation as I respond. "Now I see that the endless variety of life provides unlimited opportunities for us to evolve."

"Yes, the training grounds are individualized for every imaginable state of consciousness and can range from an entire galaxy to a single-cell life form. Now I will show you a different educational system designed for new arrivals that have exited the physical world."

I'm suddenly in a bright, classroom environment. Before me are a dozen children, who appear to be five- to eight-years old, sitting in a circle on the floor. Each child is intently focused on an object. As I survey the group, I see a boy staring at a large sphere floating before him. I watch as the color of the globe changes from bright blue to vibrant orange.

Next to the boy, a girl smiles as she changes a square building block into a rectangle; after a moment, she changes it back to a square. The teacher moves from child to child, encouraging their success and offering guidance as needed. I can sense the children's excitement as they recognize and enjoy their individual creative abilities. Watching closely, I notice that the ears and eyes of the children and the teacher differ from those of humans. Their eyes are much larger and their ears are tiny by comparison. My thoughts are interrupted.

"They are progressing well. Children are often more open-minded than adults. Their ability to shape and mold their reality is an essential aspect of their spiritual evolution. These young souls soon will soon reincarnate and return to their physical planet for further training. The density of their physical world will make the creative process more challenging for them. Your perception is accurate: they are not human. The human form is just one of billions that consciousness uses to evolve through form and matter."

As I watch, I must admire the children's natural abilities and I'm also surprised to see so many souls assuming the form of a child.

"These nonhumans died at a young age and because of this they continue to maintain their childlike appearance. All souls shape their energy bodies with their prevailing self-concept.

"Now rest; you have much more to learn."

CHAPTER 26

THE EDUCATION OF SOUL
THROUGH MATTER

Welcoming some downtime, I fall into a purple velvet chair by a crackling fireplace. I can finally relax with sips of warm chocolate and soft background music. Returning the cup to a side table, I release all thought and stare into the flames. My eyes grow heavy and close, while my arms and legs seem to melt into the fabric of the chair. It's not long before I begin to feel a familiar vibration; a buzzing starts low and then increases in strength.

My awareness separates from my body and I find myself at the top of a mountain. It's an ethereal world. A crowd of people at the bottom of the mountain stand watching. They are shouting and waving, encouraging me. The ground is pure white, but it's not snow. Effortlessly, I begin to glide around the top of the mountain; it's a wild experience. Empowered, I feel the need to travel to the bottom, but hundreds of trees block my path. With increasing speed I coast down the steep side of the mountain, easily avoiding the many obstacles in my way. It's thrilling to move and glide without the heaviness of a dense body to slow my progress.

I'm ecstatic and return to my body completely refreshed; I know that I'm progressing and on the right path. At that moment, I welcome Remi back to continue my lessons.

"Humans fail to comprehend the nature of the school they have entered. The training curriculum can last for hundreds of lifetimes. For the process to be effective, souls place themselves into a dense environment where they will accept the unfolding dramas as completely real. In this three-dimensional environment, they will experience each lesson as genuine and meaningful. Every challenge is an opportunity for soul to grow. You will now witness the magnitude of your training program through matter."

We are at the front of an ancient, domed building, reminiscent of the Parthenon in Rome. My guide's thoughts are clear and precise. "Enter with a clear heart and open mind."

White stone columns frame the arched entrance and I step into a large, domed room of gleaming white marble. The floor is made of hundreds of intricately carved stones creating a large mosaic of characters. Standing in the center of the ornate floor, I watch as a stone comes alive in my mind. That one is connected to the next and I suddenly realize that each is a physical lifetime that I have experienced. My memories form a complex, living tapestry of events. My many lives, loves, and hard-won lessons of existence on Earth come together to form this living montage. I'm observing my continuing education through time. Endless dramas are exposed; some are happy, some are tragic, but they are all me.

My mind strains to comprehend this flood of images as a hundred lifetimes stream through my awareness. Memories of life after life; it's too much to absorb. My last physical life comes into focus and my childhood is displayed like a sad movie. I try to avoid the painful memories but can't escape the images burned into my subconscious mind. Buried memories from my last life come alive.

It's a cold evening in the winter. I'm five years old and sleeping comfortably in my bed when I am startled awake by the horrible screams of my mother and the crashing sound of breaking glass. Still half asleep, I stumble to my parents' bedroom and push open the door. I see my father in a drunken rage, savagely beating my mother with his fists; my mother overturns the bedside lamp as she fights back. I stare at the bloody spectacle before me. My bruised and battered mother spots me at the door and screams, "Get help!" Terrified, I run several frozen blocks, half naked and barefoot, to my grandmother's house.

Later that night I stand shivering in the cold by my grandmother's side as I watch two policemen handcuff my drunken father and drag him to a waiting police car. A few moments later, my mother's limp and bloody body is carried on a stretcher from the house to a waiting ambulance. I run to her side and see her swollen and bruised face. Her yellow dress is spattered with blood, her eyes are swollen shut, and her nose and jaw are mutilated. Her face is so disfigured I can barely recognize her.

As the childhood images fade, a realization becomes clear: even this traumatic experience was a gift in disguise. This is a crushing reminder of the impermanence of all physical things. Of course, I was only a small boy unable to understand the events around me at the time, but I learned the importance of taking decisive personal action and becoming self-reliant. Is this not a gift? My grandmother later told me that I had saved my mother's life by running for help. Now it was up to me to save my own life. That day, the all-important attributes of resourcefulness and inner strength were just beginning to bloom. Every hardship is a potential for growth if you recognize it.

Memories of other lives thunder through my being and are unleashed in my mind. Each life offers a snapshot of the lessons learned. Millenniums of life are in me, countless stories unfolding. My mind strains to comprehend the flood of images. I realize that I've experienced countless opportunities to learn and grow. Events fill my awareness; I'm a sailor, a soldier, a farmer, a mother, a monk, and a teacher. There are too many lives to count.

I watch myself as a frail Chinese rice farmer tilling a small patch of swampy land, living in extreme poverty. Every day is a fight for survival as I struggle to support my family. I recognize that I'm completely absorbed in the basic needs of feeding and providing shelter for my family. It is a back-breaking existence.

But throughout this hard life, a single gem shines through: the love I feel for my wife and children. This life is filled with hardships but also overflows with self-sacrifice and devotion to others. My visions continue and I see a middle-aged woman in ancient Rome. I am this woman yet I also know that I'm an observer.

Pulling up the sides of my ragged dress, I adjust the dusty sandals on my feet. It's a hot summer day and I'm watching our magnificent legions marching south from their great conquest of Gaul. The pride I feel for my son, who is returning after three long years of fighting the barbarians, is overwhelming. He was recently elevated to the rank of centurion after distinguishing himself in several battles and I'm eager to see him and spend time together. I wish my husband were here to greet him, but sadly, he died of the plague the year before. I miss him.

A fresh stream of insight saturates my mind and I'm amazed at the clarity of the unfolding images. *I am a German officer during World War II, and I'm sitting in the backseat of a military vehicle moving slowly along a muddy road. As far as I can see, an endless line of gray, hollow men walks past me in the opposite direction. Their eyes are downcast; their will to fight is gone. The remnants of another defeated Russian army move slowly past me as they are marched toward the west along the side of this muddy road. They are a pitiful sight.*

I pass village after village of total desolation. Nothing lives; even the dogs have been eaten. For the last thirty miles I have smelled the decaying flesh of bloated bodies. The corpses of men and horses litter the sides of the road. The sickening stench of rotting flesh and smoke soaks my uniform and turns my stomach. Will I ever get this foul smell out of my mind? There is nothing glorious about this damn war and I fear this insanity might never end.

Though these Russians are my enemy, I can't help but feel sorry for this defeated army of lost souls. In different circumstances, I could be making this death march to hell. For the last thousand miles we have conquered all before us, but the victories have become bitter-sweet. As we move ever deeper into this barren land I can't help but wonder if we will be swallowed by this sea of gray desolation. It seems like a lifetime since I've seen my wife and child. I must shake off these thoughts of gloom; after all, we have never been defeated. The war will soon be over; we're almost at the gates of Stalingrad.

As my senses return I collect my thoughts; I'm surprised that I was a German soldier during a previous existence, yet I know that he is but a fleeting part of a more expansive me. I seriously wonder what I gained from this short and violent life. I seem to be a man in conflict with myself; I was arrogant yet showed flashes of compassion. I was a loyal soldier who would fight to the death, yet I also questioned the reasons for many things I was ordered to do. I feel a hint of sorrow for this man; he was trapped in a role he had to play out to the bitter end. How often do we trap ourselves in the many roles we play? From now on I must be careful about what roles I choose to play, and never again become a powerless pawn of my surroundings.

After I review my German life, a complex maze of other lives flashes through my awareness. The experiences form an intricate web that is difficult to comprehend. My entire perception of linear time distorts the truth: there is no time, I'm immortal. I enter and exit the dense training grounds of Earth like an actor playing on a cosmic stage. I select the learning situation and timeline best suited for the education I need. There is wisdom in this intense training. How could I ever develop the essential qualities of a mature soul, such as courage or self-sacrifice, without experiencing these attributes firsthand?

As my outer clothing of soul is discarded with each life, I see that the participants in my many lives are known to me. Like a living movie extending through time, each soul plays a part in my many physical dramas. All the characters I have known before—my mother, father, siblings, and lovers—may change the roles they play, but inwardly they remain the same immortal souls. We are interconnected.

"Your perception is accurate; souls evolve with a group they have known for many lifetimes instead of with strangers. The roles they play may change in each life but the lessons continue. You have obtained important qualities from every life. During your recent life as a German solder you experienced courage and self-sacrifice and these qualities are now a permanent part of you. Nothing is ever wasted; nothing is ever lost."

CHAPTER 27

EMBRACING THE PRESENT MOMENT

For the first time I clearly see my development through the changing dramas in matter. My entire view of evolution is transformed, and I wish I'd known this during my last physical life; I would have been far more understanding of those around me.

Remi knows my thoughts. "The human concept of time is an attempt to explain decay. The key to your evolution is embracing the present moment, for this is the only opening where you possess enormous creative ability. The past is gone and the future is but a dream. The present moment is the only reality, the single point in the illusion of time where you can shape and mold your life."

Instantaneously, I'm floating in nothingness; there are no structures, walls or floors. I feel as though I'm hovering weightless in space without a single reference point. I fight to control the waves of panic that threaten to overcome me.

My entire existence through countless physical lives extends before me, and I try to grasp the enormity of these events. It's too much to comprehend; the past and the future stretch into infinity, reaching far beyond the edges of my mind. In the distance, I see a sliver of bright white light. This shard of light becomes brighter and larger, expanding in size until it overwhelms my awareness. Drawn into this blazing light, I merge with it. I become the light of pure presence, all is clear, and the only reality is now. I finally comprehend a simple truth: only the present moment is real.

Like the sun, I radiate my thoughts outward into the external world, molding the various energies around me, and it's clear that I create my experiences through the expanse of time. My creative ability extends beyond my imagination. When I focus my full attention on the present moment, the results are dramatic; instantly my ability to create is magnified a hundredfold.

Only the present provides the opening. Why didn't I see it before? I can shape my life only in the now. Like an artist, I can create only when my thoughts touch the canvas of the present moment.

Now I understand; when my attention slides into the past, my creative power is instantly dispersed and weakened. How many times have I made the same mistake? It's up to me to learn how to direct the light of my awareness. It's up to me to take full responsibility for my thoughts and my creations.

My guide responds, "Instead of becoming a focused laser of creative light, most humans have become dim candles unable to illuminate their own path. Without the focused light of consciousness to guide them, they are doomed to wander the outer worlds as they chase their unceasing parade of thoughts.

The key to your spiritual evolution is to embrace the present moment. This is the opening to experience your true essence. Become aware every time your mind wanders from the present and is drawn to the past. Release the constant rambling of the ego's needs and the treadmill of thought. Be bold, be powerful—anchor yourself in the now."

CHAPTER 28

THE FILTER OF HEAVEN

"Clear your mind; you are ready to move on."

With a sensation of extreme inner motion, I'm thrust through layers upon layers of energy and color. It feels as if my mind is being stretched throughout the entire universe. The intense speed is impossible to describe and just as suddenly all motion ceases. My entire being bathes in the clear light of pure presence and I feel a sense of freedom I've never dreamed possible. Complete peace and harmony saturates my being.

I float in an ethereal ocean of glorious living light where my every intention manifests instantly before me. Unlimited abundance with endless levels of love and joy saturates my awareness and I comprehend a staggering truth—I possess the power of creation.

Powerful energy flows through me, and I realize that my ability to create is an enormous responsibility. It's essential for me to focus and control my thoughts, for I instantly create both heaven and hell for myself.

My guide speaks to my mind. "Your perception has grown. Imagine what one immature soul would do in this perfect, thought-responsive world of subtle, flowing energy. Picture the chaos that a single undisciplined soul could and would create. One immature soul could devastate the peaceful perfection of heaven and disrupt the privacy and joy of all the inhabitants. The purity of the higher-dimensional realities could be contaminated by a single untested soul."

The purpose for my training is now clear. The negative intentions of one undeveloped soul would pollute the perfect harmony of the higher heavens. Now I understand the intense physical training grounds of the physical and astral worlds and why it's essential for every soul to develop complete responsibility for their thoughts and deeds.

I'm brought back by the sound of Remi's voice.

"Welcome to the ultimate virtual reality, a powerful thought-responsive matrix where souls create their personal training curriculum with the energy of their own thoughts and actions. Welcome to the slowed-down molecular training ground of consciousness—the school of matter—where focused thought is required in order to create your existence. Welcome to the ideal training environment, where the young and undisciplined soul can learn by trial and error without contaminating the pure realms of spirit. Welcome to the training ground of soul—the filter of heaven."

The Earth is an effective training environment for young souls. The physical world provides the intense education that souls require to eventually coexist within the instant thought-responsive dimensions. It's absolutely brilliant: schools within schools, lessons within lessons, and all the training is self-created by the inhabitants.

"A major step to becoming an evolved soul is to master your ability to create your reality. Young, undisciplined souls are unprepared for the awesome responsibility of instant manifestation within the spiritual dimensions. Consciousness uses many lifetimes of experiences to mold the perfect creation—the spiritually evolved soul."

Now rest your mind."

CHAPTER 29

THE STRUCTURE OF THE MULTIVERSE

During my break I attempt to relax but my mind is racing; I feel as if I'm being prepared for something important. My anticipation grows and I know the answers I've searched for so long will soon be available. A soft light appears.

"Earth-bound humans remain unaware they are currently projecting their consciousness through multiple dimensions of the universe in order to experience the physical world. They have forgotten how far they have traveled to experience matter. The very process of entering and maintaining a physical body provides an essential spiritual education. Entering matter and operating a physical body teaches consciousness how to extend its awareness through the multiple dimensions of thought, emotion, and energy." Remi scans my mind and continues.

"The practice of being human is an amazing adventure—an expansive exploration of consciousness through form. It requires prolonged focus and well-developed inner energy skills to master a dense human vehicle of consciousness and fulfill your soul's purpose. Each successive energy body and dimension that soul enters provides unique training in their evolution."

For the first time I see the true nature of my education as soul. While I concentrated on the development of my mind and body

I never stopped to comprehend the mind-blowing expanse of my unseen spiritual evolution through multiple dimensions.

"Humans are so fixated on matter they see but a sliver of reality; they remain unconscious of the enormous multidimensional training ground. They believe they are in reality, when instead they are but temporary visitors in a well-designed, virtual construct created for the education of consciousness. Now you are ready to know."

I'm instantly moved into a higher aspect of myself. Floating in space, my attention is directed to the panoramic vision before me. Extending outward in every direction are thin layers of a gray, fog-like energies; layers within layers of energy and life stretch endlessly.

"A great mystery is now revealed to you. The universe is a multidimensional continuum of frequencies. Each dimension is separated by the layers of energy you see before you; each becomes progressively denser as we extend our awareness from our spiritual source and explore the outer worlds of thought, then form."

I see dimensions within dimensions, yet all occupy the same space. The beauty and simplicity is amazing, and I finally understand that I exist in all levels of the universe and they are me.

A PORTAL TO MULTIPLE REALITIES

As my perception expands, a startling new scene comes into focus: hundreds of intertwining tunnels of pulsing, white light fill my awareness and I'm moved by a powerful unseen force through a single opening. With mind-bending speed, I'm drawn through hundreds of other portals and realize that each is an entrance to another heaven, another world. Abruptly, all motion stops and I soar high above an infinite landscape of physical-like environments.

It is beyond my imagination; a thousand different realities extend outward in every direction. With some effort, I center myself and realize that each is an individual heaven and each one is separated from its neighbor by an intricate labyrinth of rivers, walls, or mountains. It's impossible to count the number of worlds that exist. Moving closer, I immediately sense that each is created by the prevailing thoughts of the local inhabitants. Each collective of souls remains largely unaware of its close neighbors and each group believes they are living in the ultimate paradise.

"Yes, you and all life forms are a part of this conscious energy system. You have the ability to navigate all the dimensions before you and become a spiritual traveler. This is your destiny as an evolved soul. Embrace it."

CHAPTER 30

SPIRITUAL NAVIGATION

I return to my body feeling transformed. As I consider my last experience, I sit on the stone edges of a clear blue pool and dangle my feet in the cool water. With small splashes, I disrupt the still water and enjoy my serene surroundings; a dozen white Roman statues stand guard around the outer perimeter of the pool. This seems to be a place that has existed for thousands of Earth years and I'm pleased to be here as I reflect on my many lessons. The last experience has changed me in ways I don't yet understand. I feel energized knowing that I'm being prepared for an even greater exploration of consciousness. My anticipation grows as Remi appears and readies me for the next experience.

"To become an effective spiritual explorer and escape the gravity of the outer worlds, it's essential to open to your unlimited abilities as soul. You have seen how humans base their entire concept of reality upon three-dimensional constructs. This single deception imprisons the human race within the outer crust of the universe. You must learn how to explore inward beyond the outer projections of form. The journey home is an inner quest through many dimensions of energy and thought. Focus, I will show you the first step for many humans."

I'm instantly inside a physical home. A young man sits in a chair and appears to be meditating; he's chanting a single sound and then goes silent. I realize I'm observing the subtle energy body of this human rather than the physical outer shell. His inner body appears as a transparent energy double, slightly out-of-phase with his physical body. I'm amazed at the complexity, as streams of energy flow throughout his body moving through several small conduits. As I watch, he goes deeper into a meditative state and I notice that the energy portals in his stomach and chest are opening, increasing the liquid-like flow of light. Each energy center appears to be alive and breathing as his body courses with currents of surging radiate light. His ethereal legs and arms begin to move and his subtle body gently separates from his physical body. Slowly, he stands and steps away from the dense body that remains sitting in the chair. He appears to move effortlessly as he glides through a wall and disappears from view. Remi's thoughts break my concentration.

"This soul is having what humans commonly call an out-of-body experience. You are witnessing the natural transfer of awareness from this soul's outer physical body to his subtle inner body. The expansive energy flow you witnessed was enabled by the life-force-transfer conduits that humans refer to as chakras. Notice that he has effectively moved his conscious awareness from one energy body to another. For many, this is the first major step in their spiritual journey. Now, prepare for your own journey inward."

I do my best to prepare myself.

"It's essential to recognize that your consciousness is the creative force behind everything. Your thoughts mold the energy around you, exerting a powerful force upon all the energies you encounter. Are you ready?"

I eagerly respond, "Yes."

I'm shifted into a higher frequency within myself. With this motion I'm floating above my body and my perception is radically changed; I can suddenly see in all directions simultaneously. At first it's confusing as the images blend together, but I slowly surrender to my expanded three-hundred-sixty-degree awareness. As I allow the images to flow, adapting to my enhanced perception, a wave of excitement surges through me. All my old concepts of vision are washed away. A bold new world opens; it's as though I've been blind my entire life and now I finally see.

"You are ready to perceive beyond form; examine your hands."

I reach out my hands and stare. To my surprise, they begin to dissolve. I can't help but smile and then laugh to myself as the instructor explains.

"Your body is a temporary energy vehicle of soul, created and maintained by your subconscious thoughts. When you consciously confront the projected image of your own thought creation it will lose its integrity, its cohesion of form."

My entire body continues to dissolve and I become what can only be described as an expansive point of crystal clear awareness.

"You have the ability to create any energy body you select. Now concentrate and create a new vehicle for your consciousness. Feel yourself becoming one with your creation."

With focused imagination, I see myself as a large golden eagle with muscular wings, beautiful feathers, piercing eyes, and sharp talons. Then I feel myself becoming this powerful bird; I spread my wings and embrace the sensation of flight. The joy of liberation surges through me as I effortlessly soar on the air currents and fly high above the green valley far below. I can feel the cool wind on my face and with the slightest motion of my wings I glide to the right and soar to the left; I'm thrilled, weightless, and my every movement is effortless. The pure freedom of flight is intoxicating. The power of creation flows through me and I know that I'm limitless; I can be anything I choose, for I shape and mold my entire reality. I surrender to the sheer ecstasy of flight and glide higher and higher, beyond all concepts of form.

The welcoming inner voice of my teacher gently pulls me back to my training. I feel refreshed and ready for whatever is next. I can sense Remi's warm thoughts.

"I also love to fly; it's one of many gifts we possess. Now focus; you are ready to experience true freedom beyond form."

A wave of excitement flows through me and I know that all of my training has prepared me for this moment.

"The human concepts of motion, time, and space are primitive. To experience liberation from the outer dimensions of form, you must learn to navigate within yourself. At this moment, you dwell within every energy level of the universe. You are directly connected to everything that is; there is no separation between you and your spiritual source." My anticipation grows as Remi continues.

"Remember, whenever you feel disoriented, you can stabilize your state of consciousness by using the focused command, '*Awareness now!*' Make this a powerful demand for immediate results. Do it now."

As I focus, repeating the command, "*Awareness now!*" my perception expands. I feel centered and locked within the present moment as a wave of self-empowerment surges through me.

"All the forms you have ever experienced are merely the outer vehicles of consciousness. These external forms of energy will melt away as you move inward within yourself. The greatest secret of the universe is you. You are the inner-dimensional portal to the entire spiritual universe. Focus on your presence. I will assist you to adjust your internal frequency."

ENTERING THE FIRST INNER DIMENSION

I'm moved to a location that appears to be my physical home before I died. I stand in my old family room, examining the familiar red-brick fireplace and dark wooden mantle. It feels strange to be here again.

"You are now just out of phase with the physical world. Your current energy body is similar to matter but is vibrating at a slightly higher frequency. Take a moment and become familiar with this vehicle of consciousness. Like all energy bodies, it automatically molds to your self-concept. Examine your surroundings and notice that this environment appears solid and stable."

I step to the fireplace and touch it; the brick feels completely real in every aspect. The surroundings structures and furniture are nearly identical to my past physical world.

"You are now observing the energy substructure of matter. This is the first subtle energy dimension that many humans experience during out-of-body adventures. It coexists with matter but functions as a separate and parallel dimension. Now examine your energy body."

I scan my body, noting how similar it is to matter. My arms and legs are solid and my body looks and feels identical to a physical body. My guide stands by my side.

"Observe the changes of your surroundings as you increase your internal frequency and move your awareness inward within yourself."

As my internal vibration increases, the familiar solid walls around me become a vaporous, three-dimensional hologram. When I attempt to touch the wall my hand moves into the energy substance of the wall. I feel a slight resistance and a tingling, vibrational sensation as my entire arm enters the wall. With a single step, I move into and through the wall. I'm thrilled.

"As your energy body increased in frequency, it also decreased in density. You have shifted your awareness inward and have moved out of phase with this outer dimension of the universe. Your personal energy density will determine what appears solid and real to you. Now focus; we will raise our vibration and explore farther inward."

As I feel my energy body's frequency increase, the vaporous walls of my surroundings dissolve around me. I'm mesmerized by the transformation.

"As you alter your personal vibration, the environment you perceive will also change in accordance with your state of consciousness. Always remember that your personal reality is always relative to the energy density of your body."

ENTERING THE ASTRAL DIMENSION

I watch as the familiar walls of my past physical home fade from view and a completely new environment comes into focus. A vibrant green field appears before me and I can feel the higher radiant energy around me. My body is lighter and my new surroundings are brighter, the colors more intense.

"You have just entered the next major inner dimension, which many call the astral. This is the destination most humans experience after their deaths, and most mistakenly assume that this is the ultimate heaven. This energy environment is created and maintained by the collective thoughts of the inhabitants."

I can barely control my excitement; it's incredible, I've moved my awareness from one energy level of the universe to another without any outward motion.

"Now you are beginning to understand the true nature of your multidimensional self. We have the ability to experience all dimensions. However, to become an effective spiritual traveler, you must learn the art of moving your awareness within yourself. No primitive external motion is required."

I step into the green field and immediately sense the higher-frequency light of this new reality.

"As you learn to consciously navigate your awareness throughout your multidimensional self, your perception and freedom will become progressively enhanced. Remember, all form is but a temporary vehicle for consciousness. You and the universe are one."

The luminous energy of my new surroundings is intoxicating. My mind is in overdrive as I soak in the vibrant energies around me.

"This dimension is far more thought-responsive than the last one we explored. This energy level is populated by billions of souls living in environments created by thought. You experienced some of these locations when we explored the afterlife of humans."

There is pause as my guide scans me.

"You possess the ability to explore far beyond the dense outer worlds. Now you are ready to experience and know your inner capabilities. The more you open to an expansion of consciousness within yourself, the more effective your exploration will become. You can move inward from one energy dimension to another by clearing your mind and opening yourself to an inner shift of your awareness. Focus your complete attention on a single intention: 'Next level now!' Do this."

ENTERING THE NEXT DIMENSIONAL REALITY

I concentrate and repeat, "Next level now!" I feel a sensation of inner motion and I'm floating within a new place. I can sense that the energy around me is lighter, brighter, even more refined. A wave of exhilaration flows though me as I realize that I've entered yet another dimensional reality. I feel empowered.

"Much of your previous training has been centered on three-dimensional constructs. Form is merely the elementary school of soul's education. Consciousness has no limit and extends far beyond the dense creations of humans."

Remi pauses and adds:

"This essential, spiritual-exploration ability is unknown to humans; they remain locked in form and fail to comprehend the awesome power of multidimensional travel. Only the spiritually evolved have mastered the skills to navigate time, space, and the many dimensions of our universe. This is the potential for all souls."

I feel an inner shift; I'm bursting with excitement but do my best to remain calm and centered as I adjust to my startling new perception. I'm a point of consciousness with three-hundred-sixty-degree awareness.

ENTERING THE DIMENSION OF THOUGHT

"Excellent. You have moved farther inward, entering the dimension of the mind. This is the inner world of pure thought. You will find that the energies here are far more subtle and fluid. In this dimension, thoughts manifest instantly."

Attuning to the dramatic change, I feel weightless, free from the oppression of density and form. My every thought shapes my immediate environment. This is shockingly powerful and I'm humbled by the awesome responsibility. I think of one of my favorite locations—the ocean with a soft, white-sand beach—and I'm instantly there. I can smell the salty ocean air and feel the warmth of the sun as the crashing waves fill my senses. I can feel Remi's satisfaction with my progress.

"You have moved inward beyond your human identity. Now you understand that there is no need for a humanoid body. Your ability to consciously travel throughout your multidimensional self is the key to being an effective spiritual explorer. You are the doorway to all dimensions and to the entire universe; you are the inner path you travel."

I'm overwhelmed; it's happening so fast that I struggle to comprehend my new capabilities.

My guide knows my thoughts and calms me. "You are ready; trust yourself. Effective navigation within the inner dimensions is achieved by consciously connecting with your spiritual essence. Self-aware souls possess no limits. You have the power to expand your inner explorations and experience the highest dimensional realities within yourself. To achieve this, you must focus on your higher self—your spiritual essence. Your intention is the driving force of your inner explorations. Now concentrate on your single intention, 'Higher self now!' Make it a powerful demand for immediate action."

I calm my mind and focus on one thought: "Higher self now!"

BEYOND THE MIND

An explosion of energy thrusts me through layers of color and blinding light. I'm drawn inward at a speed beyond all thought.

Colors flash past me as I feel my awareness stretched across the entire universe; lights within lights and levels within levels open and envelop me.

The intense inner motion abruptly stops and I realize that I'm floating in a vast sea of pure, loving, liquid light; I'm weightless. I'm like a cube of ice dropped in warm water as my outer form and thoughts melt away. All three-dimensional concepts dissolve as waves of bliss saturate my entire being. I surrender completely to the liquid light and realize that I am the light and the light is me.

There are no thoughts, no form, just pure being. All is present as waves of bliss wash over me. It's ecstasy to be, and impossible to describe.

An immeasurable, shining abyss opens and all my remaining perceptions of reality are swept away; the nothingness that I once feared is everything. I'm free to be without the anchors of thought. I'm free to shape and mold reality as I dream it. The power and responsibility are beyond my comprehension; I no longer need the vehicles of thought to comfort me.

All weight is lifted from my awareness, and as I absorb the totality of what I am, ecstasy expands though my being. I'm infinite. I float in an ocean of consciousness, and the ocean is me; I am an endless sea of pure unconditional love. All is here and now, and I'm finally home.

A soft voice echoes.

"Now you have the answer you seek."

CHAPTER 31

REVIEW: HEAVEN IS A
STATE OF CONSCIOUSNESS

My entire perception is forever changed. I realize that my death was an awakening and now I clearly see the depth of the human condition on Earth. Seven billion souls reside in a state of amnesia. During their long journeys through outer worlds of form they have forgotten what they are; they have forgotten their purpose, where they come from and where they're going. At birth, they awake in dense bodies and must adapt to their strange surroundings to the best of their ability. They assimilate into an alien environment and quickly discover the intense trials and challenges of physical existence. It can be an overwhelming experience.

Because the answers are difficult to discover, many accept the dominant belief systems of their culture and society. They are taught to have faith and believe. On their deathbeds they remain clueless of their incredible multidimensional nature and their ongoing spiritual evolution through form and matter. The afterlife remains a deep mystery cloaked in fear.

Many hope that God or the angels will somehow escort them into the mystical paradise of their religion. Instead, after death they find themselves in a place similar to their physical world; an environment created and maintained by the collective thoughts of their fellow inhabitants. Instead of obtaining spiritual enlightenment and answers, they experience a continuation of their state of consciousness. And so the cycle goes.

Since my death, I've witnessed many strange environments and behaviors. The old maxim, "as above, so below," is more accurate than I believed possible. There are millions of realities and they are all created by the thoughts of the inhabitants. I was shocked to see that people continue to live much as they did before their death; their self-created issues and imperfections continue in the afterlife. After death only the density of the body has changed; the mindset of the individual remains the same.

As I progressed in my spiritual training I was stunned by the incredible multidimensional nature of our educational process, but now I understand the deep wisdom. Each soul creates its own life lessons through the choices it makes. There is a perfect balance that's fascinating to observe; there are no mistakes because each soul orchestrates its own learning situations. Each is drawn to the people, surroundings, and events that provide specific opportunities for its personal development.

LETTING GO OF THE PAST

After death, many continue to be attached to their past physical lives and their deep-seated indoctrination. They remain attached to their physical identities and the roles they once played.

On several occasions I tried to assist lost souls by explaining that they are now in a new life and are no longer tied to the dense limits of the past. The results were dismal at best. Most wouldn't listen, and many refused to even accept the concept of moving on or changing. Essentially, they remain locked in a fixed mindset. Looking back, the same is true in the physical world.

I know from experience that it's not an easy task to discard a lifetime of beliefs; it places us in a vacuum without the comfort of a group-support system. Even so, I have learned to let go of my past and embrace change. Knowing this, I have a growing sense of self-empowerment, and the excitement of awakening to my unlimited potential. Releasing my old programming opened the door to my spiritual awakening and freed me from the heavy weight of indoctrination that had dominated my consciousness.

Looking back over my death I realize a progression of my awareness has occurred. Through extensive trial and error, I learned to transcend my limited astral body and experience the awesome nature of my multidimensional self.

My decision to explore beyond my first heaven was a major step. This opened me to incredible new insights and knowledge. I've learned to confront my fears and take complete responsibility for my thoughts and actions. I've also discovered that I shape and mold my reality in every dimension of the universe. The lessons have been intense but effective, for I know I have changed. Now I see beyond the fleeting forms around me and remain centered while moving through the raging rivers of thought.

Most importantly, I know from experience that I'm an immortal being—pure consciousness without form or limits—and from now on I embrace love instead of fear. I will not forget again.

CHAPTER 32

PREPARATION FOR REENTRY

It feels like several lifetimes have passed since my death, and after much thought and planning, I've decided to return to Earth. My education will continue and I deeply appreciate the dedication of Remi and all my guides and teachers. I've learned much and feel the need to share my training with the physical world. After extensive investigation I have found the ideal couple to be my parents; their energy dynamic will provide the opportunities I need to confront and resolve any personal limits while helping me to remember and fulfill my primary mission on Earth. The timeline, social situations, and projected interactions with my soul group will assist my purpose.

As I wait at the entry portal for my return to Earth, I'm alone with my thoughts. I'm nervous but excited about the new adventure that is waiting for me. A familiar voice breaks my concentration; it's Shiloh.

"You have done well."

"Thanks, in part, to you. I've felt your presence through many of my lessons." I'm glad to have the opportunity to show my appreciation to Shiloh before I leave.

"Spiritual boot camp is easy when compared to the intense training lessons you will experience on Earth. Few souls ever question the dense illusions that surround them and even fewer will remember their purpose or what they truly are. But I believe that you will." Shiloh's assurance gives me confidence.

Remi appears to provide some final words of advice for me. "The task before you is difficult; Earth has become increasingly unstable with constant mental diversions. Newly arriving souls are often swamped by the overwhelming external stimuli that saturate their senses. Many souls are easily swept away by intense human emotions and the demands of a dense body. Retaining the memory of your purpose will be a serious challenge. To accomplish your mission it's important to remain centered on your inner spiritual connection." Remi stops for a moment and acknowledges the director.

"Just imagine the strangeness of it all: immortal souls who possess unlimited creative power have ensnared themselves on a rock at the outer fringe of our vast universe. Always remember, you are a powerful soul creating your own reality," the director adds.

Remi nods in agreement and continues, "The souls you selected to be your parents will provide lessons in forgiveness and detachment. Your childhood will prepare you by reinforcing specific qualities you will need to fulfill your purpose. Your primary mission is to share your spiritual training and remind the Earth inhabitants that they are courageous explorers who have the ability to consciously transcend their body and obtain the answers for themselves. You have the power to accomplish your purpose."

Shiloh takes my hand and gives me a last word of encouragement. "When the harsh energies of the physical world crash down on you, go inside and connect with your higher self." She smiles, "Your portal for reentry to Earth is now open. Enjoy the ride."

PART TWO

PREPARE FOR
YOUR ADVENTURE

CHAPTER 1

THE PURPOSE OF THE PHYSICAL
TRAINING GROUND

"It is not more surprising to be born twice than once;
everything in nature is resurrection."
–Voltaire

"Everyone and everything around you is your teacher."
–Ken Keys, Jr.

The primary spiritual purpose for the school of life is the evolution of consciousness. We are all here to learn and grow from personal experience. After countless adventures in matter, a dramatic shift occurs as you recognize that your thoughts shape your reality, that you are the creative force in your own life.

This life-changing realization shakes you to the core and you realize that you are orchestrating your own physical lessons. It's you who is producing the challenges, the hardships, and the pain. It's incredible, and at first you don't want to accept it, for it's much easier to believe that outside forces or random events are to blame. How can you be responsible for all the things that happen? When you trace the cause and effect of everything in your life, you begin to see the connection: your thoughts were the ancestors to all that has appeared in your life. When this happens, you will begin to awaken from the attachment to matter and the ego mind. You realize that the myriads of form around you are but a momentary expression created by the energy of thought. You recognize that you have chosen to enter the demanding, reality-training environments consisting of matter, thought, and emotion.

At this point you desperately wish to know the unseen purpose for your lessons, your life. Your burning desire for answers becomes overwhelming and your search for the truth has begun in earnest. For the first time, you begin to comprehend the awesome personal responsibility that is in your hands. You recognize that you command a creative power when you focus the energy of your own intention. Now your every thought and deed take on a new and powerful significance.

You become aware of an incredible truth and your world is changed forever. You now appreciate that you are the architect, the creative force in your own life. An excitement flows through you as you grasp the reality of your situation: you create the wonder in your life. You create the unfolding play of energy around you. You write the script and you define the roles. Your heart awakens to the unlimited creative potential that was always within you. You view the ever-changing forms around you in a new light; this matrix of energy offers you a perfect opportunity to grow from your own experiences. A sense of liberation, empowerment, and responsibility fills you, followed by the understanding that you are the driving force of your own life.

As your awareness grows, lessons take on a deeper significance. You begin to witness the beauty of the universe. The synchronicity of spirit gives everything in your life a new meaning and purpose. You feel a reverence for all things because you know that the characters around you are important vehicles for learning expressions of unconditional love. You take a deep breath and try to comprehend it all. The awesome intelligence behind this magnificent creation is amazing to behold—you realize that all are evolving through the use of form.

Life confirms that you are personally connected to the source. It's an extraordinary system and you can't help but wonder what kind of incredible consciousness could and would conceive of this training ground.

You are open to insights that your mind cannot explain. The breathtaking beauty of the world is beyond your ability to express. You now see that you are an immortal being using dense forms of energy to evolve, and the concept of time is completely irrelevant to the process.

The school of matter is intense. You know that each soul is learning at its own pace, creating its own lessons with the energy forms around it. Souls continue to repeat their lessons until the education is complete. What could be more effective?

With this awareness, you become a mature, responsible soul who understands your mission, your purpose. You also understand that there are many opportunities to learn and you embrace these experiences when they manifest in your life. You are now fully aware of the great school of life and prepared to grow from each new adventure.

You can't explain it, but you know you are making progress. Every day, every moment in your life, is an important opportunity for further learning. As you watch the ebb and flow of events in your life, you can inwardly smile, for you are experiencing the greatest school ever conceived, the unfolding story of spiritual evolution cloaked in the drama of form. You can feel at peace with yourself, for you may not change the world, but you have changed yourself and that is all you have come here to do.

CHAPTER 2

EVOLUTION THROUGH MATTER

"All will surely realize God. All will be liberated...All without
exception will certainly know their true self."
–Ramakrishna

The physical world is an effective training ground for our
spiritual development. We learn and grow through many experiences. All the physical changes that we observe around us are the
direct result of consciousness molding form and matter. Up until
now, our education has been centered on our self-created physical dramas and lessons. This will change as we realize that we
are not our physical bodies or our ego minds. As we evolve and
awaken to our true selves, each of us will grow through several
phases.

THE FIRST STAGE: PHYSICAL GRATIFICATION

The first stage in the evolution for souls entering Earth is their
assimilation into matter.

Young souls on Earth are primarily concerned with the needs
and demands of their bodies. Survival and physical gratification dominate this state of consciousness. You view yourself as a
physical being separated from all others around you. You believe
that you are your body, completely identifying with your physical

attributes and the many roles associated with them. Your identity is based on your appearance. The desire for physical gratification is your driving need. The world around you is seen as a competitive—and often hostile—environment. In this state of consciousness, the school of matter provides intense lessons of survival and constant physical challenges.

Because you spend your life chasing the desires of your physical body, you remain unaware of your spiritual self. As your body grows old, you face powerful lessons while confronting your mortality. The natural process of aging and death is viewed as an ordeal that is to be avoided at all costs. Overall, the lessons of life are physically based during this stage because this is where your state of consciousness is focused.

THE SECOND STAGE: EGO IDENTIFICATION

In the second stage, you believe you are your ego mind as you follow its endless dictates, its likes and dislikes. The manufactured personality of the mind is accepted as the core of your self-identity. Your thoughts and emotions are the prime focus of your life and clearly individualize you from all others.

Constantly driven by the demands of your mind, you find yourself pursuing its never-ending whims. In this state of consciousness, you view yourself as superior to those who only embrace their physical identity. You think you are advanced because your mind tells you so.

The lessons are dynamic at this stage of evolution. Since you believe you are the false identity of the mind, you find yourself on a treadmill, constantly chasing the incessant demands of your ego. Your life is a perpetual search for self-gratification and the acquisition of physical things. Unaware of your spiritual essence, you readily accept whatever beliefs dominate your culture and society.

THE THIRD STAGE: GROUP CONSCIOUSNESS

Reaching out to others in the third stage, you expand your self-identity to include specific groups. You define yourself in terms of these groups. For example: I am an American, a Methodist, or a Democrat. You mentally connect yourself to specific tribes and flags and are willing to defend the dictates created by your accepted group consciousness.

You see your group as different and unique and often view yourself in competition with other groups. This man-made division leads to separation, conflict, suffering, war, and devastation on a global scale, as there is a driving need to reaffirm the superiority of your group over others. In this state of consciousness, you often believe that you are part of the chosen group.

Because so many souls remain unaware of their true identities, they cling to the perceived security of an established group consciousness. There is safety in the herd. This can be an extremely dangerous and potentially volatile state of consciousness. Each group feels the need to defend its principles and beliefs and all too often tries to convert or eliminate all those who are different. Historically, this has led to extreme nationalism, religious intolerance, and the destruction of civilizations.

THE FOURTH STAGE: SOUL AWAKENING

In this next stage, through vigorous personal trials and challenges, you begin to recognize the illusions in the world around you. You realize that you are more than your rambling mind or your physical body. You awaken to the fact that you are a powerful spiritual being having a temporary physical experience. This is a major shift of consciousness and is often considered to be the opening stage of self-realization.

You no longer follow the dominant doctrines of society or the endless drives of the ego mind. In fact, now you can observe the antics of your mind like an unruly child who is always striving for attention. You know that spirit dwells closer than your own beating heart, so why would you waste your time looking for God outside of yourself? The truth is now evident. You realize that you are always connected to the source and that the spiritual path is within you.

THE FIFTH STAGE: PROFOUND PERSONAL SPIRITUAL EXPERIENCES

The fifth stage is where a critical progression occurs. You make the essential leap of consciousness away from dependency upon beliefs, and you experience your own authentic spiritual adventure. Then all perception is changed and you are forever transformed. The world of matter is seen as the outer vehicle of soul—a dance of energy. You know that you are pure spirit, always connected to the source within you. You understand that you are inseparable from the universal ocean of unlimited love and abundance. Your inner connection to your spiritual self becomes as essential as the air you breathe.

At this point, you awaken to your true self and you are ready to graduate from the demanding school of matter. The unfolding physical dramas of consciousness are recognized for what they are—soul evolving through the use of form. You emanate love to all, for love is all that flows within you. You are finally free from the dense, outer training ground of matter and are now prepared to enter the more thought-responsive realms of the inner dimensions. Unknown to many, this is just the beginning of your extensive multidimensional training.

THE EVOLUTION OF SOUL BEYOND THE PHYSICAL

The death of our physical bodies is just the beginning of our ongoing education into other dimensional realities. This amazing process extends far beyond the basic training on Earth. Our evolution is an inner journey of consciousness into the spiritual source within us. As we progress, each dimension we enter provides new and expanded lessons. Our training continues beyond the linear concepts of time, space, and form, and each nonphysical environment we experience provides expanded opportunities for our spiritual growth. Life and evolution continue into progressively more thought-responsive realities.

THE STAGES OF OUR EVOLUTION AFTER DEATH

Each inner nonphysical dimension we experience will provide different and unique opportunities for us to learn and evolve. The following is presented as a brief overview.

- Learning to adapt to our subtle astral body and assimilating within a new energy reality.
- Experiencing and learning within the diverse realities and training grounds of the astral dimension.
- Cleansing our astral body of the many fears, blocks, and limiting emotional patterns and subconscious drives we continue to hold.

- Developing our astral body and its capabilities by experiencing multiple energy simulations (personal fear and limit confrontations).
- Developing our subtle inner senses and the full potential of our astral body.
- Learning the essential navigation skills to explore multiple astral realities.
- Consciously exploring the astral dimension. Becoming aware of the many diverse heavens/belief territories that populate this vast dimension.
- Awakening to the temporary nature and educational purpose for all form-based realities.
- Becoming fully aware that we are the creative force responsible for shaping our reality in all dimensions.
- Learning to consciously manipulate and manifest the energies of thought.
- Opening to our inner light and love. Practicing unconditional love to all.
- Accepting our complete responsibility for all of our thoughts and actions.
- Navigating the diverse nonphysical realities of the astral dimension and functioning effectively in both consensus and non-consensus environments.
- Learning and experiencing methods of exploration to expand our awareness beyond the limits of our astral body.
- Consciously transcending the limits of the astral body and experiencing our higher-frequency, thought-energy body.
- Exploring and becoming familiar with our mental body and the corresponding dimensional realities.

- Cleansing our mental body of all the fears and limits that potentially hinder our spiritual evolution.
- Consciously mastering our expansive mental-energy body and its immense creative capabilities.
- Learning to skillfully navigate within the instant-thought-responsive realities—the higher heavens.
- Learning to consciously experience the spiritual realities beyond the mental dimension.
- Mastering our unlimited creative abilities in all dimensions.
- Mastering ou`r ability for spiritual/multidimensional travel within ourselves.
- Consciously reuniting with our spiritual essence beyond all form and thought.
- Becoming a spiritual traveler; the evolution of soul beyond all form-based concepts.
- Being a highly evolved soul who possesses the ability to consciously experience the entire expanse of the multidimensional universe.

As consciousness, we will continue our inner journey and eventually reunite with our spiritual essence beyond the confines of form and thought. There are no limits and no end point to our spiritual evolution.

CHAPTER 3

STATES OF CONSCIOUSNESS IN
THE AFTERLIFE

The individual and collective states of consciousness that exist in the afterlife exceed our wildest imagination. Group thought creates all afterlife environments, so the afterlife that an individual will experience will be the result of his or her state of consciousness. Like a powerful energy magnet, people are automatically drawn to like-minded souls and the resulting afterlife environment. Each heavenly environment is a direct reflection of consciousness held by a group of souls.

Since our state of consciousness has a direct impact on what we will experience after death, it's important to focus on and enhance our mindset and spiritual development. The following is a small sampling of the diversity found in the nonphysical dimensions.

THE ATTACHED AND UNAWARE

Those who accept only matter as valid will continue to dwell as close as possible to the physical world, even after death. Their attachments, addictions, indoctrinations, fear of change, and physical self-identities bind them to the only reality they know and understand. The end result is that many souls are drawn to the energy dimension closest to matter. This is a parallel energy dimension existing at a different vibrational density and just out of phase with the physical world. Their continuing focus upon the physical world binds them to this and other shadow environments close to the Earth. What they experience after death are energy replicas of their life on Earth. They will often ignore all offers of assistance or guidance.

THE SLEEPERS

These are souls who exist in denial of their death and remain in a comatose state of consciousness for an extended period. This is sometimes due to intense trauma or shock at the moment of death. Many souls require an extended rest-and-restoration period before continuing their spiritual journey. Since we are immortal, the length of time this process may take is meaningless.

THE ADDICTS AND OBSESSED

Even though they are aware they have died, many souls remain psychologically bound to a host of drives and addictions. During their physical life, they were obsessed with food, drugs, alcohol, sex, money, gambling, or any of the many addictions that influence the physical world. After death, their psychological desires continue to drive them. Every form of obsession continues after death because it is created and sustained by the mind of the individual. The human personality imprints persist, and ingrained obsessions are sometimes even magnified after death. Like-minded individuals are often drawn together within a consensus reality and resume their obsessions. Even death itself does not provide escape from the obsessions that influence us. This is why the great spiritual teachers from every culture have stressed the need for nonattachment to all things.

THE RELIGIOUS FOLLOWERS

Souls who retain strong religious beliefs are drawn to and cloistered within a collective reality of similar minds. Every Earth faith, past and present, can be found, and each group is highly individualized and built upon the collective consciousness of the group. Manmade beliefs dominate this state of consciousness and manifest a firmly structured, form-based reality. These are generally pleasant environments that are often dominated by beautiful replicas of earthly landscapes with massive, gleaming cathedrals, churches, and mosques. Prevalent within the astral dimension, realities of this kind are highly resistant to individual creative thought. After death, many believe that they have entered the ultimate heavenly reward promised by their religion and they quickly adapt to the consensus norms of their new surroundings and group belief system.

THE HEALERS

Many new arrivals require extensive rehabilitation, counseling, and energy work to adjust to their new frequency body and environment. Talented, loving souls assist the new arrivals to overcome the physiological issues they have carried over from their last physical life. The astral dimension provides extensive rehabilitation centers designed to support those souls who have had a traumatic physical life and death. Energy healers and environments are designed to treat every imaginable form of psychological damage incurred during the past physical experience. Infant-care and preschool facilities help the young adjust to their transition after death. The enormity of this effort is impressive. Millions of compassionate and loving souls devote their existence to this critically important work.

THE SEEKERS OF INTELLECTUAL KNOWLEDGE

These are individuals who focus on their intellectual development and the acquisition of information. Many are drawn to the continuing education of their minds, believing that they can comprehend the nature of the universe and themselves through the power of logic. They often appear in campus settings that provide every imaginable aspect of intellectual training. An extensive curriculum is available in the astral dimension. This is created by the collective consciousness of scientists, scholars, researchers, and all those who continue to rely on the intellectual pursuit of knowledge.

THE ARTISTS/CREATORS

There are souls who are learning the essential skills of creation by practicing and perfecting their individual art form. The thoughts of artists, sculptors, and other visionaries are manifested through magnificent displays of every imaginable expression of creativity. The art of conscious creation is an essential skill of an evolved soul. Every soul must become completely responsible for its thought creations in order to enter and coexist in the subtle, thought-responsive worlds within the higher dimensions.

THE SPIRITUAL SEEKERS

These are the ones who actively seek to experience enlightenment and liberation from the outer dimensions of form. They are developing their ability to unite with their spiritual essence in full consciousness, expanding their inner exploration skills beyond the limits of their minds. They are learning to explore their multidimensional selves through spiritual experiences. These souls employ different methods of inner exploration, such as deep meditation and explorations of consciousness beyond their astral bodies. They are seeking conscious union with their spiritual essence.

GUIDES AND HELPERS

The diversity and complexity of guides and helpers are as extensive as the states of consciousness they serve. They assist the living and the dead to deal with all manner of personal development, challenge, and ultimately—a soul's spiritual evolution. They assist the transition of souls and the movement of consciousness from one energy level to another. Generally, they are specialists in specific areas of soul development. For example, some assist individuals in their spiritual quest to confront and dissolve their fears, overcome self-made limits, and become more aware of their unlimited potential as soul.

SPIRITUAL TEACHERS

These beings assist others. They provide the training needed to enhance our spiritual awareness, qualities, and skills, allowing us to transcend the shackles of form. The underlying goal of all instruction is to teach souls how to navigate their multidimensional selves and experience the magnificence of their spiritual essence. The first part of this book provides a window into some of the developmental training that can be found. Remi would be one example of a spiritual teacher.

SPIRITUAL TRAVELERS

The enlightened ones are graduates of the intense training in the physical and astral dimensions. They are highly advanced souls who have evolved beyond the influence of ego and the need for form. Spiritual travelers are consciously aware and have mastered the skill of self-directed and controlled multidimensional exploration. They possess the ability to explore all time lines and experience all of the many dimensions of the universe in full awareness. Travelers have complete freedom to explore levels of creation far beyond human conception. As pure consciousness, they are formless but have the ability to create and utilize form-based constructs as their vehicle of expression when required. In biblical literature, these highly evolved souls were often thought to be angels. We are all in the process of potentially evolving into this unlimited state of being.

CHAPTER 4

DEVELOPING YOUR CREATIVE ABILITY

One of the essential skills we require to become a mature soul and coexist in the higher, thought-responsive dimensions is our innate ability to create our reality. Ask yourself an important question: in a world where every thought becomes an instant reality, who would you want standing next to you? We have learned that all physical objects, including all life forms, are multidimensional and composed of nonphysical energy. However, what many do not see is the extent, depth, and critical importance of this discovery. Few realize that the physical world is but one of many training grounds for developing souls.

The universe is much like a multidimensional hologram of energies molded by the power of thought. The physical world we see around us is the thin, dense, outer crust of this massive energy projection. The creation of form begins within the subtle inner core of the universe and flows outward from the spiritual source into the progressively denser vibrations of thought, emotion, and finally, matter. This magnificent hologram of energy is always ready and able to respond. In fact, the universe has always responded to your personal thoughts, but it is up to you to learn how to control and focus your own projections of thought energy.

The bottom line is this: thoughts are things, and we mold our reality. We create it by the way we project our thoughts and intentions both consciously and subconsciously. Every limiting and negative self-concept, belief, and falsehood hampers and blocks our creative flow. It's up to each of us to awaken and learn how to manage the powerful creative flow of energy within ourselves. Until we take complete responsibility for our own energy creations, we will remain cloistered in the dense, outer training schools of the universe; we will remain in the physical and astral dimensions. The great spiritual teachers throughout the ages have repeatedly taught the truth of this but few have listened.

THE KEYS TO MANIFESTING YOUR REALITY:

1) RECOGNIZE THAT EVERYTHING IS A FORM OF ENERGY.

Modern physics has proven that everything around us is a form of moving, subtle energy; nothing is truly solid. Also, science has confirmed that all energy, even subatomic particles, can be influenced by thought. In fact, a child's thoughts can alter the motion of subatomic patterns. This knowledge opens the door to a startling new vision of reality and our ability to influence it.

2) KNOW THAT WE MOLD OUR INDIVIDUAL ENERGY REALITY WITH THE FOCUS OF OUR INTENTION.

Every physical object begins with a focused thought. Your thoughts create the energy molds commonly called thought forms within the inner dimensions. The key is to not only think about your goal but also to commit it to writing. Be specific. Writing your specific goals or dreams helps to crystallize them even faster. In addition, it's helpful to create a detailed manifestation or a vision board that displays pictures and photos of your personal goals.

3) CREATE A MENTAL MOVIE.

Create a detailed mental movie of your new life as you enjoy and interact with your dreams. Imagine and feel yourself currently enjoying your creations now.

4) TEST-DRIVE YOUR INTENTION.

As an example, if you desire a new car, physically test-drive the one you would like. If you want a new home, go to open houses and do a walk-through. Feel yourself owning and enjoying your dream now.

5) TAKE ACTION WHENEVER POSSIBLE

This is the step that many seem to overlook. Look for opportunities for you to take action to manifest your dreams, even small things are important in the creative process. There is no coincidence, so become aware of the small changes or openings for manifestation that are occurring in your daily life.

6) BE OPEN TO RECEIVE.

The final step is to be completely open, without conditions. Don't prejudge the outcome of your goals, for they will often manifest in a different form than you may have envisioned. A powerful phrase to repeat is, "this or something better will appear in my life now." In addition, express gratitude for all that you receive, even the small things.

The creative end result is clear, our focused intention and action mold our reality; however, wishing and hoping does not. Each of us possesses the power of creation in our lives, but it is up to us to use our inherent ability. Our focused intention creates a subtle energy mold within the inner dimensions, and our individual thought forms are the birthplace of our reality. The proper use of this knowledge creates a powerful life-changing shift in consciousness that will transform your life.

When you take complete responsibility for your thoughts and actions and embrace your natural ability to create your reality, all things are possible. Be empowered, embrace your personal creativity and consciously build your life today. To explore this topic in more detail, see *The Secret of the Soul,* chapter nine. Please refer to the diagram titled, The Energy Mechanics of Creation, for a description of this universal creative process.

CHAPTER 5

OBSERVING YOUR THOUGHTS

"No one saves us but ourselves, no one can and no one may."
–Buddha

The truth does not care what we choose to believe—it remains unchanging. It is up to each of us to take responsibility for our own state of consciousness and experience the truth within. As seen through the story of Frank's afterlife experience, our physical self-conception, indoctrination and dense limits are carried with us and even magnified after death. That is why it's so important to recognize and remove as many energy blocks as possible during our current life.

We who see so little of the vast universe are often quick to create and hold firm convictions about everything. For many people, an effective way to enhance our self-awareness is through the dispassionate reappraisal of all of our beliefs and conclusions. Why do you believe what you do? What evidence supports your conclusions? Listed below are some of the states of consciousness that can prolong our spiritual journey through matter. Take a moment and answer each question with detailed responses, and objectively examine your personal library of beliefs.

Allowing beliefs to dominate our mindset: Take a moment and examine your personal philosophies. Do you believe that you are the victim of fate or do you know that you create your own reality? Do you that believe you are a powerless, sinful being that requires an external force to save you? Do you believe in eternal hell? It is up to us as spiritual beings to empower ourselves to experience the truth of existence, for we possess the ability to experience our spiritual essence and obtain the answers we seek. Are you ready to take complete responsibility for your current state of consciousness and make the changes needed to enhance your self-empowerment?

Allowing the ego mind to dominate our consciousness: Examine your thoughts several times during the day; notice any repetitive ideas and how they influence your behaviors. Ask yourself the following questions throughout the day: What is driving my daily activity? What motivates me? Am I experiencing a treadmill of recurring thoughts and actions created by my ego mind? What can I do today to break my old habits of thought and action?

All manifestations of fear: Our fears, both conscious and unconscious, create the invisible cage we live within. Our fears limit not only our physical life but also our continuing existence beyond the body. After death, our current state of consciousness lingers and our negative or limiting energies are carried with us. This is one of the primary reasons why most of humanity will experience the limited consensus realities within the astral dimension after their death. We have the God-given ability to alter our current life and our spiritual path. Begin to deliberately notice the nagging little fears that inhibit you from achieving your spiritual goals and confront this restrictive energy whenever possible. What are you afraid of? Why? What small actions can you take now to overcome your fears today?

Attachment to any physical object, relationship, or location is an anchor to matter and inhibits our spiritual progress: Most people, even after death, continue to be attached to the roles they once played: mother, father, gender, race, and even the role of human. Do you believe you are your body? Are you attached to a physical identity that will potentially limit your spiritual progress after your death? Are you ready to open your mind to a more expansive vision of yourself?

Attachment to any psychological or physical addiction: Ask yourself this: Is there anything to which you are currently attached or addicted? This is a time to be completely clear and honest. Recognize that our psychological baggage—our obsessions and dependences—continues beyond the physical. What actions can you take today to free yourself? Create a list and make a personal commitment to confront and resolve each issue as soon as possible. Design your own action plan.

Holding on to negative emotions, such as anger, resentment, or guilt: Emotion is a powerful form of energy. Today there is considerable attention given to forgiveness of others, but little is said about forgiveness of self. Ask yourself, do you continue to feel any resentment, guilt, or anger for a past event in your life? What action can you take today to release yourself from the negative energy you may hold?

Attachment to the past: How often does your mind wander from the present moment to replay earlier events? How much of your valuable creative-thought energies are drained into the past? Do an exercise for one day: Monitor your thoughts and every time your mind wanders to a troubling situation from the past, catch yourself, acknowledge it, and immediately let it go. Our thoughts possess immense creative power; the manner in which we focus our thoughts will determine our reality now and in the future. Like an artist, you can craft your life only in the present moment; take control of your creative-energy flow now and consciously build your life.

If any of these issues apply to you, confront and resolve them. Several times during the day, become the silent watcher of your recurring thoughts and habits. Become aware of your repetitive inner dialogue. The first major step to self-empowerment is to shine the light of your awareness on the issues you need to address. Create a personal action plan and every time you recognize a personal energy block to your potential, neutralize it by sending light to the situation. Become aware and feel a shift of consciousness occurring within you. Recognize the change.

CHAPTER 6

TECHNIQUES FOR CHANGE

"Holding on to anger is like drinking poison
and expecting the other person to die."
– Buddha

Belief reappraisal, daily meditation, inner energy work, focused intentions, and many other spiritual practices can have a positive impact on our states of consciousness. In addition, self-initiated out-of-body experiences can provide a powerful opportunity for a profound spiritual experience and awakening. Refer to *Adventures beyond the Body* for more details. The following are a few simple methods to reappraise and enhance your journey.

UNCOVERING THE INDOCTRINATION THAT HINDERS OUR SPIRITUAL GROWTH

Few people stop to consider that their library of cherished beliefs was never their own. They live within the narrow confines of the established thoughts and conclusions created by the minds of others. Most take their lifetime of programming for granted as a normal part of our socialization process. Even the clothes we wear, the style of our hair, and the types of food we eat were created by others. How often is your life manipulated or limited by the ideas of others? How often do you accept an established belief or concept to fit in?

Every unconfirmed idea, limit, and belief is a potential mind trap hindering our personal and spiritual development. From this moment, take notice of the many external forces that are attempting to influence your state of consciousness. Any thought or idea that contains a form of limitation or fear-based manipulation is a mind trap. A lifetime of physical indoctrination has an enormous impact, for our minds are filled with thousands of assumptions that create our limits, our fears, and the invisible walls we experience in our life.

This goes far deeper than most would begin to imagine. The very basis of human civilization is the firm, undisputed conclusion that we are physical human beings; yet countless out-of-body and near-death experiences confirm that we, as consciousness, possess no biological or humanoid form. In fact, as we prolong an out-of-body experience our outer human form dissolves away and we become a sphere or pinpoint of consciousness existing beyond all density and form. In other words, our human body is but a temporary and expendable vehicle of our true, nonhuman spiritual essence. If the foundational belief of all human civilization and thought is completely flawed, then just imagine how many more of our conclusions are also false? The bottom line: question everything.

From this moment, notice the thoughts that limit your full potential, every time a thought begins with: "I can't," "I should not," "I should," "I must," or "I am not able, or capable." Become aware of the restrictive thoughts that are imposed on your mind and your life. Question everything. Only we can break the cycle of conditioning that restricts us from achieving our full potential.

CALMING THE SEA OF THOUGHT

Calming the mind is the first step. To begin, imagine that you are sailing on a small boat in the middle of the ocean. The waves are turbulent, rocking you from side to side. Feel the motion of the ocean moving you. These waves represent your busy, rambling thoughts. We have the ability to quiet our minds and completely relax.

Take several deep, cleansing breaths. With each exhale, imagine and feel the surrounding ocean becoming smooth as glass. Watch the ocean waves subside, and feel that you are becoming completely calm and centered. With each inhale, feel relaxation flowing through your body and mind. Clearly imagine that all motion has ceased and your mind is drifting in a state of complete peace. Feel yourself becoming still and weightless, floating in your body.

OBSERVING YOUR LIFE

Sit quietly and observe a typical day in your life. See yourself as you wake in the morning and move through your daily routine. Recall how you interact with others and how you set your priorities. As objectively as possible, examine and observe your life: scan your daily habits, thoughts, and attitudes.

Are you on a treadmill? Are you experiencing a repetitive loop of daily thoughts and actions? What unresolved fears or issues may be holding you from achieving your potential? Are you procrastinating decisions and actions? Are you pursuing your dreams and passions or are you in a holding pattern? Only you can answer.

Imagine what comments a spiritual guide, like Remi, would make while observing your daily life? What kind of example would you be to other souls? If the answer is not what you like, now is the time to change your habits and your life. At this moment you have the power to transform your entire life direction by just making the firm decision to do so. Only you can do it. Empower yourself to make the changes you need, to be the best you can be.

BECOMING THE WATCHER

An effective method to evaluate your personal progress is to step back and watch your reaction to the many interactions you experience during the day. For one full day, check in every hour and briefly observe your dominant thoughts and emotions. How do you mentally and emotionally feel throughout the day? What thoughts are you projecting on a daily basis? Every emotion and thought is a form of energy and your daily life is your spiritual training ground. Our family members, friends, and work associates often offer the greatest challenges to our state of consciousness. How do you respond to daily issues? How do you respond to any form of unpleasant behavior directed toward you during the day? Do you respond in kind, with a negative thought or word, or do you let the energy move through you without offering any resistance?

Recognize the many opportunities for personal growth that are present in your daily life and become more aware of your reactions to all the energies that swirl around you; practice daily non-attachment. Practice the art of being transparent and at peace with yourself regardless of the external events unfolding. This may be one of the easiest ways to appraise and enhance our state of consciousness. Make it fun and become the objective spiritual watcher of your mind.

CREATING YOUR PRIMARY SPIRITUAL INTENTION

Most people drift through life without ever considering their ultimate spiritual goal. They remain completely immersed in the daily drama of their physical lives while the critical importance of their spiritual development is completely overlooked. Let us change this now.

Take a few moments to focus on your ultimate spiritual intention. Ideally, what do you wish to experience and achieve in this life? Self-realization? God-consciousness? Union with your higher self? Use terms that you feel best clarify your personal intention. Make this your focused, spiritual goal.

Our spiritual evolution is the powerful unseen engine that drives our lives. It orchestrates the personal lessons, dramas, conflicts, and the relationships we need to learn and evolve. For many, physical existence is a challenging journey of self-awakening.

A boat without a rudder will drift and founder in the ocean. By focusing on our spiritual intention, we begin to steer our journey of consciousness and accelerate our spiritual growth. One easy method of focusing our intention is to create a clear affirmation and repeat it several times a day, like a mantra. For example, repeating "higher self now" or "spiritual essence now" can be powerful. Silently repeat your affirmation as you are drifting to sleep or while meditating. Do this for several days and notice any vibrational changes or shifts of perception occurring in your state of consciousness. Often, your entire being may feel lighter and brighter. Repetition of your spiritual intention as you drift to sleep can also initiate lucid dreams and out-of-body experiences. Ideally, hold your intention as your last thought as you go to sleep.

CARVING YOUR PRIMARY SPIRITUAL INTENTION INTO YOUR MIND

Close your eyes and become centered. Calm your mind and imagine that there is a large block of stone before you; this stone represents your subconscious mind. Picture yourself carving your focused, spiritual intention into the stone. Use the present tense; for example, "Now I experience my spiritual essence." Clearly picture yourself carving each word with a chisel or power tool. Feel it manifesting before you. Step back and view your creation. See, sense, or feel it clearly. Acknowledge that you have just carved your spiritual goal into your mind. Absolutely know that your focused, spiritual intention has become a permanent part of your conscious and subconscious mind. Now accept and embrace your focused intention as an essential part of your complete being. Repeat this visualization until it becomes second nature to you. Do this daily and, preferably, before your daily meditation and out-of-body exploration sessions.

PEEL THE ONION—A GUIDED MEDITATION

Take several deep, cleansing breaths and imagine and feel a calming, white, vibrant light flowing down from above and entering the top of your head...

The relaxing light is gently moving through every cell and system of your body and mind ... Feel yourself relaxing with each exhale. Every nerve and muscle is letting go, relaxing...

Now imagine that you are peeling away all of the outer, dense layers of your life... your possessions, your house, your car, your personal belongings, your clothes, your furniture, and all of the objects and structures that surround you...One by one, feel all the objects around you dissolving away.

Allow yourself to let go of all of your possessions... and as you do, feel you are becoming lighter... Peel away all the things you own or possess, all the things you have labeled as yours...

Now feel your body dissolving away and fading from view... Take a deep breath and feel your body becoming lighter and lighter...

Peel away all of your emotions, thoughts, feelings, likes, and dislikes; remove them all... Feel you are becoming lighter and lighter as you strip away the outer facade of density and form... Peel away all of your ideas, conceptions, and beliefs... Take a moment and let them go...

Now, surrender and release every belief and conclusion you have accepted since childhood; seek them out and cast them off... Feel yourself becoming lighter and lighter as all of the outer parts of your mind are peeled away... Release your memories and your personal history; let them all go... Peel away all of the events you are attached to, all the connections, all the relationships. Let them go...

Feel yourself becoming lighter and lighter as you let go of your past and all of your thoughts and ideas... Peel away all three-dimensional concepts, all dense self-identities...You are becoming lighter and lighter, letting go of all attachments to form...

Release all of the concepts of the human form, releasing all identification with three-dimensional forms... Peel away all of your outer form, all of your thoughts, all of your emotions.

Let go of any lingering residue of a physical self-concept... Release all of your beliefs... Feel yourself letting go... You are feeling lighter and lighter; you are pure awareness without form...

As you peel away each layer of matter, thought, and emotion, something remains... awareness that existed before your body, before your thoughts, emotions, and possessions...

When you peel everything away, one perception remains: pure awareness... You are clear, conscious light with the unlimited ability to create anything that you focus on... Becoming lighter and lighter as you merge with the clear light of awareness... Surrendering, you become the pure light of awareness... weightless, effortless... Feel yourself floating, free of all density and form... Become one with your spiritual essence...

Surrender and embrace the joy of pure being.

THE SPIRITUAL HEALING VORTEX—A GUIDED MEDITATION

Take several deep, cleansing breaths and allow your eyes to close.

Imagine a powerful vortex of vibrant, healing, white light above your head.

This spinning vortex of energy has the ability to heal your body and mind.

Clearly imagine and feel this spinning vortex of energy slowly descending and entering the top of your head.

Feel this vibrant healing energy moving through your head and shoulders, cleansing every cell and system of your body.

The powerful light is moving down through your chest, stomach, and hips, releasing all fears and limits.

Imagine and feel that your arms and legs are becoming lighter and lighter.

Feel this spiraling energy vortex moving through and enveloping your entire body.

You can sense and feel that you are floating and weightless as all negative vibrational energies are transformed and removed from your body and mind.

Completely surrender to the swirling, healing energy and feel the difference.

Sense and feel the vibrant healing energies moving through you.

Release all thoughts that no longer serve you. As you do, feel yourself becoming lighter and lighter.

Silently repeat these affirmations as you surrender to the healing energies:

"I open and allow the pure light and healing love of God to flow through me."

"I open and allow all my energies, thoughts, and emotions to be transformed now."

"Now I release all energies that no longer serve my spiritual growth."

Feel and sense this happening now…

Become one with the healing energy moving through you.

Embrace the lightness of your being… Let go and flow.

FIRE CEREMONY

Fire is the ancient, universal symbol for transformation. For tens of thousands of years, shamanic cultures have practiced a fire ceremony to release their fears and enhance their reality. During my workshops, I use a fire ceremony to focus our intention, allowing us to be open for positive changes and shifts of energy in our lives. Over the past twenty years of conducting this ceremony, I've witnessed amazing results and personal miracles. A shortened version of this ceremony can be practiced at your home. A fire source can be a fireplace, wood stove, candle, or even an outdoor grill.

First, clearly visualize the changes you would like to manifest in your life at this moment. Create a brief written list of the primary life changes you desire immediately. Place each intention for change on a separate piece of paper. Concentrate on the most important energies, relationships, or situations you would like to manifest in your life now. Focus on the underlying energy of your intentions. For example, a new car may symbolize increased personal freedom.

After writing your specific intentions for change, verbally affirm that you are completely open for the transformation to occur in your life now. Make this a firm commitment for immediate personal change.

Take a moment and imagine your current daily life with your changes in place. Ideally, create a vivid mental movie of your new life situation. Vividly see and experience yourself now enjoying your new reality. Make this personal movie as detailed as possible.

After affirming your complete openness to these changes, place each written intention into the fire and acknowledge the immediate energy transformation in your life as each intention burns to ashes before you. Feel the energy shifting as you repeat, *"I am open and receptive to these changes in my life now!"* Reaffirm that you are open to receiving your specific changes in your life now. Imagine and feel it happening now. Give your sincere thanks and gratitude for the new energy flow now occurring in your life. Be open to immediate change. *"I give thanks for what I now receive. Now I am completely open and receptive to these changes in my life."* Before, during, and after the fire ceremony, remain open to experience the changes immediately. *"Now I'm open to these changes in my life. Now I express my gratitude for what I receive."*

It's essential to focus our thoughts on the energies we wish to manifest in our lives. Every focused thought has creative power, so direct your thoughts with extreme care.

OPEN TO HEALING

Lie still in a quiet, comfortable position. Close your eyes. Breathe deeply and state your healing intentions to the universe. Picture in your mind the base (root) chakra. See it begin to spin faster and faster until it is sparking with energy. Subsequently, move up through each chakra (sacral, solar plexus, heart, throat, third eye, and crown). Feel them spin. They begin to light up and you can feel the pulsing strength increasing with each breath.

Now open your crown chakra and invite the healing power of the universe into your body. Feel it flow up and down the length of your spine, spreading through your shoulders and down your arms to the ends of each finger. Feel the healing energy move down through your chest, flowing past your hips, down your legs, and to the tips of your toes.

At this time, visualize all parts of your body working in perfect harmony. You can focus on a specific area (My bones are strong and healthy... My mind is sharp...My memory is flawless). You can visualize general health (I have a healthy, fit body). Once you have completed your own healing, send it out to others you have in mind. Again, you can focus on an individual, a group, or on mankind in general. This process is especially powerful if done during an out-of-body experience.

OUT-OF-BODY EXPERIENCES AS A SPIRITUAL PRACTICE

I strongly feel that one of the most effective ways to prepare for our transition is to learn about and practice out-of-body exploration. Self-initiated OBEs provide vital firsthand knowledge of our nonphysical energy bodies and prepare us for the many thought-responsive realities we will all enter at death. Ultimately, our personal experience is our greatest teacher. I have covered this important topic extensively in my previous books.

CHAPTER 7

SPIRITUAL EXPLORATION MINDSET

The single most important issue we confront in spiritual exploration is our ability to create and maintain the ideal mindset. During our inner explorations we experience nonphysical dimensions that are extremely responsive to thought; these subtle energies will respond to our subconscious and conscious thoughts with amazing speed. Our thoughts function as a powerful creative force that will often manifest form-based projections. Over the years, I have come to realize that this is a critical issue that is seldom addressed. For example, if you believe in a devil, demons, or evil aliens, you may experience an energy manifestation or projection of your own deep-seated fears. Sacred texts from many different cultures and religions provide clear examples of this energy-manifestation process in action. I explore this important topic in detail within, *The Secret of the Soul*, Chapter 8.

Focusing on our spiritual intention and developing the ideal mindset is essential in our inner explorations of consciousness. The following knowledge has greatly assisted me in my personal explorations and in my daily life. I question everything and assume nothing. I have found that cultural and religious beliefs, assumptions, and our own physical self-conception can act as anchors that hinder our spiritual progress. The following are my personal reality principles; please accept or reject as you like.

1. I am pure consciousness. I possess no form or three-dimensional structure. I have the ability to manifest and use different energy forms for my expression and education. I realize I am not humanoid or any other form-based concept.

2. I am immortal, creative, and powerful; nothing seen or unseen can harm me or block my spiritual path.

3. I shape, mold, and interpret all realities. I create my reality both in and out of body. I accept complete responsibility for all my energy creations for I'm the creative writer, director, and actor in every drama I experience. My consciousness uses form like a master puppeteer.

4. I am an explorer of consciousness and seek the answers to life's mysteries. When I expand my explorations inward beyond all form-based realities, I possess the innate ability to obtain the answers.

5. I remain open to my unlimited potential and independent from all belief systems, religions, and consensus-reality conclusions. The truth is not man-made.

6. My natural perception is 360 degrees. I remain alert to the fact that I actively color, shape, and mold my perceptions. All the realities and life forms I encounter are interpreted by my mind. I realize that my consciousness is highly interactive in all energy environments.

7. I remain calm in the face of intense vibrational shifts and manifestations. To the best of my ability, I remain detached and neutral to the various energies that I encounter. As much as possible, I am the objective, dispassionate observer of the unfolding imagery, concepts, forms, and dramas that I experience.

8. During all altered states and shifts of consciousness, I remain completely calm and centered.

9. I am open to and embrace unconditional love in my life and reject all manifestations of fear.

10. I possess no limits; I can move, expand, and express my conscious awareness without limit. I create the limits or blocks that I experience, so I can dissolve them.

11. I control my state of consciousness by using focused, powerful commands: Awareness now! Higher self now! Next level now! Clarity now!

12. I demand to experience my higher self whenever possible. I expect immediate results and clear answers now. As much as possible, I surrender to my higher self, to my inner guidance. I trust my higher self, for I am my own guide.

13. I currently maintain and operate a personal energy vehicle (body) within every dimension of the universe. I have the natural ability to shift my conscious awareness throughout these energy bodies and experience and explore without limit. I travel the inner path within me. I experience and explore the entire multidimensional universe within myself. External motion and energy forms are unnecessary. The direct path to self-knowledge and self-realization is within me.

14. To the best of my ability I identify, confront, and resolve my fears both in and out of the body. I realize that my fears will manifest as form-based energy and blocks. I actively seek to dissolve all the fears I experience.

15. The key to self-knowledge is to expand my spiritual experience. I aggressively examine and purge all unconfirmed

conclusions, concepts, and beliefs from my mind. The lighter I am, the further inward I can experience.

16. All form-based realities are temporary energy constructs. Form is created and shaped by consciousness. I seek to experience and comprehend the true source of all realities.

17. Attempting to comprehend and navigate the multidimensional universe using any belief system as a guide leads only to extreme self-delusion, recurring blocks, and deception. I follow my inner wisdom, my higher self. I am the path I travel.

18. To uncover the truth of my existence, I must explore beyond matter and form. True reality and answers exist beyond the three-dimensional energy forms of the astral and physical dimensions. I consciously embrace the higher realities deep within me.

19. I remember my inner explorations and obtain the answers I seek.

20. I encourage and embrace radical and rapid change and remain completely open to experiencing accelerated personal growth. Mental stagnation and rigid thought patterns are not an option.

21. The key to achieving accurate perception is to examine and cleanse the lens of my mind so I am free from the indoctrination and self-deception that dominate all form-based realities. Clear perception is essential and it is my complete responsibility.

22. I am the one who creates and maintains any blocks to my progress. I take complete responsibility for my life and my experiences.

23. My life experiences provide the lessons I designed for my education. I always dig for the unseen reason and educational purpose behind my experiences.

24. "Awareness now" is my focused intention and my silent mantra.

25. I have the ability to navigate, observe, and explore the entire multidimensional universe and all time lines.

26. I focus on the now, for I can create and manipulate my reality only in the present moment. Now is the focal point of all my creative energy. My access to immense creative power dwells in the now.

27. I assume nothing and question everything. I realize that all form is a temporary reality; it is an expression and tool of consciousness. I confirm the authenticity of all the life forms and realities I encounter.

28. I recognize the importance of transcending all external methods of perception, including the powerful tool that is my mind. Transcending the mind is essential in order to truly perceive the profound nature of my higher self.

29. There is no separation between myself and enlightenment.

30. I have found it extremely helpful to maintain a detailed dream journal. It helps to condition and open my mind to accept and experience multiple realities.

31. Confronting and dissolving the energy manifestations of my own fears, limits, and blocks is essential for my spiritual growth. There are no negative experiences, only energy manifestations that I currently don't comprehend.

32. I don't waste my energy promoting or defending my perceptions of reality. I realize that those of us who know from experience will understand.

33. I expect profound spiritual experiences NOW.

I highly recommend creating your own ideal exploration mindset list. The very process of writing your personal list can expand your mind. Do it today.

CHAPTER 8

FACILITATING AN ENLIGHTENED

TRANSITION

"O nobly-born when thy body and mind were separating, thou
must have experienced a glimpse of the pure truth…"
—*Tibetan Book of the Dead*

Let's face it: most people are afraid to die. They possess no solid evidence of what is on the "other side" and they are hoping and praying that heaven is a reality. Unfortunately, for millions of people approaching death, the lack of personal knowledge about the afterlife leads to overwhelming levels of fear and anxiety. It does not have to be this way.

In our modern society, those approaching death are often sent to a professional facility to die "in peace." The primary emphasis of the family and the medical profession is on patient comfort and pain control, while the critical importance of the transition of consciousness at death is completely overlooked.

Hospice caregivers and nurses do a tremendous service to humanity but are often extremely limited in presenting any information that might be perceived by family members as a form of religious instruction or guidance. Every year, millions of people are essentially left to die alone in medical institutions while being cared for by complete strangers. We have the ability to do so much more to assist our loved ones and ourselves during this important part of our evolution.

Ultimately, the task of assisting ourselves and our loved ones to experience an enlightened transition will be our responsibility. We have the innate ability to do so much more than provide physical comfort; we can assist by focusing our attention on the potential for our spiritual empowerment during the process of death. To do so, however, we must become more aware of our capabilities and be prepared to take the appropriate action.

THE TIBETAN BOOK OF THE DEAD

An ancient approach to assisting the transition of consciousness has become all but lost in our modern culture. For many hundreds of years Buddhist monks have sat at the side of dying people while chanting powerful mantras to assist the individual to make an enhanced spiritual transition of consciousness to the higher spiritual realms. This spiritual training was provided within an 8th century text titled, *Bardo Thodol*, translated, *The Great Liberation Upon Hearing in the Intermediate State*. Today this book is commonly called, *The Tibetan Book of the Dead*. This revered manuscript teaches that once the soul is freed from the body it can experience several different nonphysical realities or bardos. It instructs individuals how to go to the higher spiritual dimensions instead of stopping at the lower vibrational realms (the astral plane) where the cycle of reincarnation continues. The individual is guided to navigate through the denser (lower) nonphysical environments of the astral dimension and experience the highest vibratory level of reality that they are able. In this ancient text, the core philosophy for assisting the dying can be distilled into one powerful mantra; "Go to the clear light of the void." In perhaps a more modern context, "go beyond the astral dimension—unite with your spiritual essence".

It's important to note that the word, "hearing" is an intricate element of the title. The Tibetan monks understood that we could influence the important transition of consciousness called death, and that the dying person was capable of hearing and responding to our guidance. They also understood that the transition of consciousness was a continuing process of spiritual evolution even after death. This is why the term "intermediate state" denotes that other shifts of consciousness will be experienced while soul is in the afterlife.

DIRECTING A CONSCIOUS TRANSITION AT DEATH

When confronted with the possibility of my own death, I created a personal plan to enhance my transition. I knew from forty years of out-of-body adventures that the focus of my awareness is critical to the results I experience during all states of consciousness. During my OBEs I discovered that I'm a multidimensional being and my awareness is a continuum of consciousness currently dwelling within all energy levels of the universe. From experience I learned that focused commands can greatly influence the destination of the nonphysical environment I encountered. For example, during an OBE, the firm command, "Next level now" can propel our awareness inward to a higher frequency (less dense) energy environment or dimension.

During my workshops, I teach a simple method that can assist us before, during and after the transition of death. First, create a clear, focused affirmation of your ultimate spiritual goal. Then, silently repeat, "Spiritual essence now!" or "Higher self now!" Or whatever terms that resonate with you. To the best of your ability, maintain your highest spiritual intention and goal as your last conscious thought while you drift in and out of consciousness. Ideally, have friends and loved ones around you who will reinforce your spiritual intention through verbal and silent affirmations.

ASSISTING A LOVED ONE TO REMOVE THEIR FEAR AND FOCUS ON THEIR ULTIMATE SPIRITUAL GOAL.

If possible, discuss with your loved one the many benefits of approaching the transition of death with a focused spiritual intention. Instruct them to be crystal clear about their ultimate objective.

As you sit with someone who is approaching death, guide them through personal affirmations to focus on their core spiritual self. Direct them to go beyond all three-dimensional realities. Focus on their natural ability to reunite with and experience our spiritual essence, our true self. Use terms that are meaningful to the individual and absolutely know that your uplifting guidance will be effective. Through repeated, loving, verbal reminders, encourage them to reunite with their spiritual essence. An effective approach is to repeat the affirmation, "Now you go to (experience or reunite) with your Higher Self." Depending on the circumstances this guidance may be silent or verbal.

At the deathbed of a loved one, offer suggestions that will encourage the individual to release all fear and attachments and experience the spiritual core of their consciousness. As much as possible, use terms that will be understood by the individual but keep in mind that your clear spiritual intention is more important than the words you use. Simply talk to the person about the unlimited potential of their spiritual nature. Assure them that they have the natural ability to experience immediate spiritual growth and enlightenment. If your personal presence or verbal communication is not possible, directing focused thoughts or prayers to the individual can also provide assistance. At the end of this chapter, I have listed some sample affirmations.

SPIRITUAL GUIDANCE AT THE TRANSITION OF DEATH

To begin, say a brief, calming prayer or meditation to center and open yourself to the unlimited power of the universe flowing through you. Ask to be a clear, receptive channel for the power of God. "Now I am a clear open channel. The power of God flows through me!" Allow the inspiration, thoughts, and words to stream through you.

Focus on the positive aspects of the approaching adventure in consciousness, the potential spiritual awakening, the unlimited love and freedom that are now available to all of us. Guide your loved one to seek and experience the pure spiritual essence of their being. Use phrases that will denote pure spiritual awareness to the individual. Gently instruct the individual to release all their personal fears and attachments while embracing the unlimited freedom of their spiritual self.

In addition, it's important for the individual to release any and all forms of negative energy they may continue to hold, such as hatred, fear, resentment, and anger. It's equally important to forgive yourself and others of all the conflicts or issues that may remain unresolved. "I sincerely forgive and release (name of person or group) completely and forever. I'm free and I set free all who may have harmed me during my life." Repeat an affirmation or mantra that focuses the person on their ultimate spiritual goal. Make this clear and concise, and use the present tense. Use terms that will resonate with the individual. Ideally, maintain this guidance before, during, and for some time after the transition is complete.

Most importantly, as you feel yourself approaching the transitional point, focus and maintain your undivided attention upon a powerful affirmation that focuses your full awareness upon your ultimate spiritual essence or goal. Make this statement a powerful mantra in the present tense. "Now I (or name of loved one) go to my higher self!" or "Now I experience my spiritual essence!" When assisting a loved one, repeat their name and use phrases to fit the social situation. At the end of this chapter are a few examples. For more detailed information about this important topic, please refer to Chapter 8: *A New Vision of Death and Dying,* in *The Secret of the Soul.*

Listed below are some questions I often receive during this important discussion.

If my loved one is unconscious, can they still receive spiritual guidance? Yes. The subconscious mind will still receive the guided assistance even if the body is influenced by narcotics or in a coma.

How long after the transition should I continue the affirmations? Use your intuition to determine the appropriate length of time. Two days may be right for some, others may go longer. In some eastern traditions individuals and groups will repeat their "spiritual release" meditation or prayer every day for 21 days.

Should I stay with my family member continuously?
This is a personal decision. For many, the practical approach is to create their own affirmation audio recording that will provide some level of spiritual assistance and guidance so it will be available on a 24-hour basis.

What is the most important element of this process? Your focused and uplifting spiritual intention is the most important aspect. Keep your terminology simple and easy to understand. Focus on the state of consciousness of the individual, not the surrounding emotional and physical issues. Many people are more focused on the flower arrangements than the all-important spiritual transition of soul.

Does the guidance need to be verbal? This is not essential but it is recommended if the circumstances allow it. Many people practice verbal guidance combined with focused silent prayer and affirmations.

Do you feel that cremation is beneficial? Yes, it helps to break the deeply entrenched mental and emotional attachments we hold to our physical body and to our fleeting physical existence. In many cultures and religions, the severing of all physical attachments is considered essential for the continuing evolution of soul. This is the primary reason why more than one billion Buddhists and the Hindus practice cremation. Few people ask an important question: How can we expect to enter the higher spiritual dimensions when we remain mentally attached to our physical body and our past physical life? Choose well.

AFFIRMATIONS FOR AN ENLIGHTENED TRANSITION

One powerful method of enhancing the transition of consciousness is to incorporate spiritual affirmations as a mantra. Select the affirmations that focus on your highest spiritual intention. Repeat and hold them as your last conscious thought. Another approach I highly recommend is to record your selected affirmations and create an audio file or CD to play when appropriate. Have a loved one do this for you if you not able. Select the affirmations that resonate with you and record them over a selection of music you find inspiring and relaxing. Play this recording at the bedside during your own or a loved one's pending transition. Program your audio device for repeat play at a soft volume.

When making your recording, use phrases that focus on your personal spiritual goals, enlightenment, self-realization, or whatever terms represent this concept to you. The goal is to focus your entire state of consciousness upon your spiritual essence beyond all form-based realities at the moment of death. One approach is to record your affirmations in both first person and second person, i.e., "now I" and "now you." Repetition of the phrases is intentional. (I consider this so important that I have recorded my own custom audio program for myself and my family members.) Spiritual self-empowerment through our personal intention is an effective way to accelerate the evolution of our consciousness. The terms God, source, or universe may be interchanged, depending upon your personal preference. The following are examples;

I encourage you to create and use your own focused spiritual affirmations.

- o Spiritual essence now!
- o Now I reunite with my spiritual source.
- o Pure, unconditional love fills my entire being.
- o Now I experience my higher self.
- o All my fears are now washed away.
- o I am immersed in the love of God.
- o I embrace joy and love throughout my entire being.
- o I am open to the unlimited love of God now flowing through me.
- o I am completely safe, secure, and loved.
- o Now I forgive everyone, including myself.
- o Unconditional love flows through me.
- o Now I release all attachments to form.
- o All of my fears and limits are dissolved away.
- o Now I enter the clear light of the void (all Buddhist and Hindu variations).
- o I'm completely loved and accepted.
- o I embrace my spiritual essence and release all attachments.
- o Now I become one with my spiritual essence.
- o Now I'm filled with pure light, pure love.
- o I am an open channel for the love of God.
- o Now I go to the clear light beyond all form.
- o Now I become one with my higher self.
- o The unconditional love of God fills me.
- o All of my fears are washed away.

o I embrace joy and love.

o I am open to the unlimited love of God flowing through me.

o Now I experience my higher self.

o I am completely safe, secure, and loved.

o Now I forgive everyone, including myself.

o All my attachments to matter and form are released.

o Unconditional love flows through me.

o Now I experience my spiritual essence.

o All of my fears and limits are dissolved away.

o Now I enter the clear light of the void.

o I am completely loved.

o I embrace my spiritual essence and release all my attachments to form.

o I am pure light, pure love.

o I am immersed in the pure love of God.

o Now I go to the clear light beyond all form.

o Now I merge with my spiritual source.

o I accept the unconditional love of God.

o Now I experience pure awareness beyond all form.

o I am the pure light of God.

o I go beyond all form and experience my spiritual essence.

o Now I release all attachments with my past.

o I am open to experiencing my spiritual self.

o The love of God (universe) surrounds and protects me.

o I forgive all; I release all.

o Now I release all attachments to my body.

o I accept the unlimited power of love in my life.

o I am pure light and love.

o Now I embrace the present moment.

o   All of my fears and limits are washed away.

o   Unconditional love surrounds me.

o   Now I experience my spiritual essence.

o   I embrace the love of God.

o   I surrender to my spiritual essence.

o   I release all my fears and limits.

o   Unconditional love fills me.

o   I release all attachments to form.

o   Love expands through me, love envelops me.

o   I reunite with my spiritual essence.

o   The love of God fills me.

o   I am pure love and light.

o   Now I experience my spiritual source.

o   Higher self now!

By incorporating our spiritual intentions into our lives we have the ability to assist ourselves and others to experience an enlightened transition. It's important to create a dialogue with our loved ones and ideally create a detailed action plan for your own spiritual transition. Our focused spiritual intention is the key. As highly creative souls, we have the ability to direct and enhance our state of consciousness. No excuses; for it's up to each of us to awaken and empower ourselves to experience our full spiritual potential in our current life and in our afterlife.

CHAPTER 9

QUESTIONS AND COMMENTS

WHAT IS THE BIBLICAL HEAVEN?

The biblical concept of heaven was an early attempt to describe the many magnificent unseen energy dimensions that exist beyond our physical vision. In general, heaven is a series of subtle energy environments that are highly thought-responsive and are molded by the thoughts of the inhabitants. Millions of nonphysical realities exist and the variations of these "heavenly" environments are unlimited. Many of these could be perceived to be a biblical paradise.

WHAT DOES THE AFTERLIFE LOOK LIKE?

Each individual will experience the afterlife that resonates with his or her individual state of consciousness. Even though the number is unlimited, most people will experience physical-like environments that are comfortable and familiar to them. Many people who have had near-death experiences recall environments that are more vibrant and beautiful than their earthly counterparts. An all-pervasive and loving light is said to saturate the higher-frequency realities. Gardens, parks, oceans, deserts, universities, libraries, churches, rivers, and mountains have been described. Groups of souls that share a collective vision often experience surroundings that are similar to their previous existence on Earth.

Evidence strongly suggests that most astral inhabitants remain cloistered within a relatively limited, physical-like environment. There are countless magnificent nonphysical realities; however, we will experience the one that resonates with our individual state of consciousness.

WHY IS OUR SPIRITUAL DEVELOPMENT DIFFICULT AND APPEAR TO TAKE SO LONG?

Souls visiting Earth love to weave their intricate web of dreams out of form and substance. A dilemma unfolds, because we become attached to our own creations. Our continuing attachment to the physical world often slows our spiritual development. This applies to both the living and the dead, because souls continue to be attached to their human form even after death. How do you teach humans that their cherished body is not their true self-identity, just a temporary vehicle of soul? How do you prove to them that they are not physical creatures? How do you show them that they are immortal spiritual beings who exist within multiple dimensions? How do you convince humanity that they can explore beyond their bodies and obtain the spiritual answers for themselves? The evolution of soul is a demanding process because each individual makes it so.

WHAT IS DEATH?

Death is a natural transition of consciousness to our higher-vibrational energy body. At the moment of death, we experience the transfer of our consciousness from our dense outer vehicle (the physical body) to our more subtle (astral) energy body. We are immortal as soul, so death is the ultimate illusion.

WHAT WILL MY NONPHYSICAL BODY LOOK LIKE?

After death most adults will appear as a younger version of their past physical body. The nonphysical body is extremely thought-responsive and will automatically assume the self-image held by our conscious and subconscious mind. It's common for nonphysical residents to appear to be in their prime of life, with a continuation of the last physical gender, race, and personal identity.

WHAT IS THE PURPOSE OF THE HARDSHIPS OF THE PHYSICAL WORLD?

The primary purpose for experiencing the physical world is the evolution of the consciousness. The essential qualities of an evolved soul are developed through extensive personal experiences. The physical world provides this intense educational environment in order for souls to learn through firsthand experience. When the qualities of an evolved soul (love, compassion, fearlessness, self-sacrifice, etc.) are acquired, the soul is then capable of coexisting within the highly thought-responsive dimensions beyond the astral dimension.

Training young souls within the physical and astral dimensions is a universal and highly effective process. When the training is complete, the fully tested and mature souls are then energetically prepared to enter and experience the instant-thought-responsive realities of the higher spiritual dimensions.

IS REINCARNATION REAL?

Yes. The education of soul through repeated experiences in the physical world is a common method for spiritual evolution. Reincarnation is essentially a training system for consciousness; this process has proven to be extremely challenging but also highly effective. Graduates of the physical training ground are highly regarded as spiritually evolved souls.

WHAT ARE THE SECOND AND THIRD HEAVENS?

There exist countless vibrational realities. After a person's initial entry and orientation into their first "heavenly" environment, some awaken to the fact that other realities are available. These souls will eventually explore beyond the consensus limits of their peer group and seek to experience higher heavens. As we raise our state of consciousness, exploring inward beyond the first energy body, we have the ability to experience higher-vibrational environments (heavens) within the astral dimension. As a side note, most religious texts, including the Bible, the Koran, and the Tibetan Book of the Dead, refer to multiple heavens.

WHAT IS THE SECOND DEATH YOU TALK ABOUT?

The second death is the shedding of our current astral body and the movement of our conscious awareness into our higher-frequency energy body. An example is presented in part one; immediately before Frank enters his spiritual training, he experiences a second death and subsequent rebirth into a higher-frequency energy body. We are all active participants in a multidimensional, soul-development process. Our education and evolution continues through many different vibrational-energy bodies and within the corresponding realities.

DO ALL SOULS EXPERIENCE THE PHYSICAL WORLD?

No. Our entrance (incarnation) into the physical dimension is always our choice. No one is forced into a physical body. We possess the free will to decide our personal path of evolution. Many souls consider the physical-reality training of Earth to be far too extreme, and choose to evolve in other dimensional-energy systems such as the astral.

IS EARTH THE PRIMARY PHYSICAL TRAINING FOR SOULS?

No. Our planet is but one of countless inhabited worlds used for the evolution of soul. Consciousness uses every imaginable energy body and life form to evolve itself. Once entered and assimilated into a given reality, most souls will return to the same energy system, such as Earth, during their training and education. Other souls incarnate in different planetary systems and use diverse biological bodies to evolve their individual states of consciousness. The wide spectrum of consciousness inhabiting the universe requires multiple vehicles of expression, and many of these are beyond our current comprehension. The use of temporary three-dimensional bodies is but one of the many tools employed by consciousness for its primary goal of spiritual evolution.

WHAT IS REALITY?

Reality is relative to the observer's state of consciousness and the frequency (density) of its current energy body. Form-based energies that coexist at the same vibrational rate or density as the local inhabitants will be perceived as its reality. To truly understand the nature of reality, we must expand our mind beyond the perceptions of form and density. For example, countless realities exist beyond our three-dimensional concepts of substance and form.

WHAT IS A SOUL GROUP?

This is a collective of souls who are evolving together through multiple experiences within the physical and astral dimensions.

Many souls choose to evolve through the hardships of the physical world with a select group of spiritual friends and acquaintances instead of complete strangers. Members of soul groups share individual and collective aspirations for their spiritual growth. The core-soul-group number varies widely; however, groups of twenty to forty individuals are not uncommon. There is increasing anecdotal evidence that primary and secondary soul groups exist.

HOW CAN I BEST PREPARE FOR MY DEATH?

First and foremost, enhance your state of consciousness by releasing all negative energies such as anger, resentment, jealousy, and hatred. Second, as you approach the point of transition, focus on experiencing your spiritual essence by mentally repeating a powerful affirmation, "Higher self now!" or, "Spiritual essence now!" Make this your focused personal mantra. Refer to Part Two, Chapter Eight, *Enlightened Transition*, for more details.

CAN WE RELY ON BELIEFS?

No. Our best approach is to free our minds of all manmade beliefs and seek the truth of our spiritual existence. It's up to each of us to explore and experience our spiritual essence. One of Jesus's most profound statements is clear, "Seek first the Kingdom of God". He never taught, "Believe in or pray for the Kingdom of God." Pursuing our personal spiritual experiences is absolutely essential in our evolution as soul.

WILL I EXPERIENCE A NEW OR RESURRECTED SPIRITUAL BODY AT DEATH?

The concept of a born-again or resurrected body is inaccurate; each of us already possesses a subtle astral body that is an essential component of our multidimensional nature. When we shed the physical body at death, we simply transfer our conscious awareness from the outer physical body and experience our subtle astral body. Death is the natural shedding of our dense vehicle of consciousness.

DO WE RECEIVE THE ANSWERS TO LIFE'S GREAT MYSTERIES AFTER DEATH?

The dead do not magically become all-knowing or spiritual. At death, the individual's state of consciousness remains the same; only the density of the energy body is changed. Essentially, the narrow-minded and ignorant remain so after death and continue their journey of personal development through many lives and experiences. It's up to each of us to enhance our awareness and develop our full potential as immortal souls.

WHAT HAPPENS AT THE MOMENT OF DEATH?

At the moment of death, we experience the natural transfer of our consciousness from the physical body to our existing, subtle astral body. Most people are immediately met by loved ones who are a part of their extended soul group. Generally, each person is reunited with a collective of souls that shares his or her mindset and stage of spiritual evolution. Souls will automatically experience the physical-like environment within the astral dimension that corresponds to their vibrational (spiritual) development.

WHO OR WHAT CREATES REALITY?

All realities are the direct result of consciousness. Each non-physical environment is molded and maintained by the collective thoughts of the local inhabitants. Groups of like-minded souls often join to create a collective vision of reality. The very act of shaping our personal environment with our thoughts (creation) is an essential element of our spiritual training. As soul, we possess this creative power in every dimension.

ARE WE MET BY ANGELS OR JESUS AT DEATH?

At death, people are met by members of their soul group (familiar loved ones and peers). We will likely be met by individuals we know who are equal to or close to our state of consciousness and spiritual development. If your personal state of consciousness and spiritual development is equal to that of Jesus, Buddha, or the angels, you might experience their realities.

WHAT IS THE AFTERLIFE EXPERIENCE FOR MANY SOULS?

The afterlife provides every imaginable form of entertainment, interest, and method of creative expression and personal development. All forms are widely available, with music, art, and theater being major preoccupations for many souls. The essential skills of creation and healing are developed through the manipulation of energy. Advanced and innovative methods of construction, architecture, science, and the manifestation of art through form are practiced by many. Anything that we can imagine can exist, for all creation is achieved by focused thought. Each soul pursues his or her selected hobbies, sports, art forms, and recreational interests. For those seeking personal growth and spiritual development, no limits exist except those created by each soul.

WILL I MAINTAIN MY SAME STATE OF CONSCIOUSNESS AND PERSONALITY AFTER DEATH?

Yes. Your personality imprints and state of consciousness continues after death. Whether ignorant or enlightened, you will continue your individual path of spiritual evolution and development. Only the outer body will be changed; the mindset of the individual remains.

DOES TIME EXIST?

Time is a human creation to track energy changes and the deterioration of matter. What is time to an immortal?

HOW DO WE COMMUNICATE AFTER DEATH?

All communication is by direct, thought transference. This is a far more effective and elegant form of communication than crude physical language. The nonphysical body does not possess biological vocal cords, ears, or eyes. We communicate through our thoughts and emotions, both conscious and subconscious.

ARE THERE CHILDREN IN THE AFTERLIFE?

Yes, after death, a child's self-identity will continue to mold his or her own subtle energy body. Most children will experience their astral bodies as the same age and gender that they were on Earth. The education and guidance of children is a major endeavor in the astral dimension and many souls devote their existence to the care, nurturing, and education of children. This is a highly regarded labor of love. As children grow in awareness and maturity, their energy body will also change to reflect their state of consciousness.

HOW DO SOULS SPIRITUALLY PROGRESS AFTER DEATH?

First and foremost, we progress spiritually by breaking free of the massive physical indoctrination and dense limits we carry with us. We progress by systematically purging our subtle astral body and our mind of all negative energies such as anger and fear. We can also advance through selfless, dedicated service to others. Most importantly, we evolve by consciously connecting with our spiritual essence. Our personal spiritual experiences are the essential key to our spiritual evolution within every dimension of the universe.

ARE THERE CHURCHES AND RELIGIONS IN THE AFTERLIFE?

Every state of consciousness and belief system continues in the afterlife. Souls are drawn to those of like mind, often recreating the environments and structures that are familiar to them. All religions continue in the astral dimension in some manner. Often the core doctrines are adjusted to meet the aspirations of the specific group consciousness. For example, the role of Jesus is often reframed from a God-like image to that of an advanced spiritual soul existing in a higher dimension beyond most souls' current reach. As souls evolve spiritually, the need for primitive man-made creeds and doctrines naturally drops away.

WILL MY CURRENT RELATIONSHIPS CONTINUE?

A strong bond of love and attachment in the physical world is likely to continue in the afterlife. However, each individual is faced with a choice whether to maintain any and all social interactions.

It's common for primary-soul-group relationships to continue in some form.

AFTER DEATH, DO WE FUNCTION LIKE WE HAVE A PHYSICAL BODY?

Most people will continue to maintain their physical-like identities and capabilities. The nonphysical body we experience at death is a thought-responsive structure consisting of subtle energy and is molded by our mindset. As nonphysical beings, we no longer possess biological vehicles of expression; we do not breathe air, require sleep, see and hear with physical eyes and ears, or evacuate waste. However, billions of souls residing in the astral dimension will continue to eat, sleep, and do many physical-like activities out of habit. As we grow in spiritual awareness, our attachment to our physical self-identity diminishes and our creative abilities as an immortal soul become enhanced.

IS THERE SEX IN THE AFTERLIFE?

Yes, however, it's different than in the physical world. Nonphysical sex within the astral dimension is more of an energetic melding of conscious energy. Many describe it as a merging of emotional energy that is far more intense than physical sex— like a full-body orgasm of the mind.

DO WE HAVE SPECIAL ABILITIES AFTER DEATH?

That depends on the personal limits held by each individual after death. Most people are creatures of habit and will remain psychologically attached to their physical self-concept and limits. The more spiritually advanced will experience greater freedom of mobility and be able to move beyond the confines of a single reality. The evolved soul can project its awareness into multiple, dimensional realities, transcend all barriers, and can interact and communicate with higher-evolved beings. Our abilities as soul expand exponentially as we connect with our spiritual essence and release our physical indoctrination. As we grow spiritually, we naturally become more aware of our unlimited multidimensional abilities and expand our knowledge and our access to higher-frequency realities.

DOES ETERNAL HELL OR DAMNATION EXIST?

No. Spiritual evolution, not punishment, is the underlying principle of our existence. All afterlife environments, both positive and negative, are formed by the consciousness of the inhabitants. Because of this, there exists an extreme diversity of energy realities. All souls have the ability to elevate their state of consciousness and transition to higher-frequency environments. Reality in every dimension, including the physical, is always in a state of flux and can be changed by the spiritual progression of each individual. Since we are immortal, the length of time this process of spiritual evolution may take is meaningless. Eventually, all souls will become enlightened, even if it takes millions of Earth years. This is the brilliant design of our magnificent universe—the spiritual evolution of soul through extensive personal experiences.

YOU OFTEN TALK ABOUT ENERGY CONSTRUCTS AND SIMULATIONS. WHAT ARE THEY?

Essentially, they are crystallized thought forms and events made manifest by individuals and groups. Constructs are thought forms that possess a three-dimensional energy structure and are perceived as a solid reality by the observer. Simulations are energy events—dramas that create the learning opportunities for soul within every reality. Often, these energies will manifest as personal challenges that must be resolved to learn something and move forward in life. Afterlife realities are less dense and more thought-responsive than the physical, so these energy constructs and simulations can manifest exponentially faster than matter.

WILL MY SURROUNDINGS BE PHYSICAL-LIKE AFTER DEATH?

Yes. After death, our immediate nonphysical environment and body can be as real and solid as the physical world is to us now. Our energy body and our environment will consist of a form of subtle energy and frequency that is less dense than the physical.

HOW DO WE SPIRITUALLY PROGRESS AFTER DEATH?

Many are surprised to learn that the process of spiritual development continues much the same after death; only the density of the environment has changed. To begin, it's important to cleanse our astral body and our mind of all lingering negative energies. What fears, guilt, anger, hatred, and attachments do you continue to hold? It's vital to practice effective methods to have profound spiritual experiences so we can expand our conscious awareness beyond the confines of our current energy body and connect with our true self—our spiritual essence.

It's also essential to open our minds and acquire accurate knowledge about our continuing spiritual evolution through form-based realities. Part One of this book explores in detail the topic of spiritual training and development after death.

WHAT DIMENSION WILL I EXPERIENCE AT DEATH?

Most of humanity will find themselves living in physical-like consensus realities located within the astral dimension. We are drawn to the energy reality that most resonates with our individual state of consciousness and self-identity.

WHAT IS THE PURPOSE FOR MULTIPLE ENERGY BODIES?

They allow us, as soul, to enter and experience multiple energy dimensions of the universe. All energy bodies, including the physical, are temporary vehicles of consciousness used for the exploration and expression of soul. They provide the essential method required to experience and learn within the many energy dimensions of our universe. In order to function within each dimension, we require a body that is in vibrational sync with the local energy environment. For example, a physical body is needed to interact in the physical world; the same applies to all other energy dimensions. Pure consciousness or soul exists at a much higher vibrational frequency than matter. Soul uses progressively denser energy bodies (subconscious, mental, astral, and physical) to step down its high frequency and enable it to extend its awareness and function throughout the entire universe. This brilliantly conceived system is the core spiritual dynamic allowing consciousness the ability to interact with, and evolve within, the many energy levels of the multidimensional universe. Temporary energy bodies, such as the physical, are the fundamental method soul uses to express itself in all dimensions and spiritually evolve through intense personal experiences.

WILL I EXPERIENCE MY SOUL AFTER DEATH?

Each of us will experience the energy body and vibrational reality that is in sync with our state of consciousness; the vast majority of humans will experience their astral bodies and reenter the astral dimension. Soul exists at a much higher energy frequency than the astral body and few people today have enhanced their state of consciousness to the spiritual level of perfection (self-realization or enlightenment). Those rare individuals who have become spiritually enlightened during their physical lives will experience the higher-frequency levels of the universe.

It's important to understand that we are multidimensional beings currently functioning with many different vibrational energy bodies. Our astral body is not soul; it is our subtle energy body closest to the density of matter. When we shed our outer physical bodies, we shift our awareness to the next subtle energy body we already possess.

WHY ARE OUT-OF-BODY EXPERIENCES IMPORTANT TO OUR EVOLUTION?

How do you truly know something unless you experience it? What better preparation can there be for our transition than our firsthand experiences beyond the body? OBEs provide a powerful confirmation of our immortality, the removal of fear, and invaluable insights into the nature of our multidimensional spiritual selves. They also allow us to experience and adapt to the thought-responsive realities we will enter at death. According to many hospice workers and nurses, it's natural for individuals close to death to report spontaneous out-of-body experiences that include detailed communication and visitations with dead relatives and friends.

Based on all the available evidence, I feel strongly that self-initiated out-of-body experiences are an ideal way to prepare the dying for their new spiritual reality. It gives them an opportunity to adjust to their new nonphysical environment and adapt to the thought-responsive capabilities of their astral body. In a very real sense, it's the natural way to introduce each individual to the nonphysical world they are about to enter. It does not matter what religious beliefs you may hold; there is no escaping the fact that you will have an out-of- body experience and enter a new energy reality beyond the physical. Something this universal and important to your future deserves your attention. Please refer to *Adventures beyond the Body* for the many benefits of out-of-body experiences.

WHY IS DEVELOPING OUR CREATIVE ABILITIES SO IMPORTANT?

It's essential for each of us to master our creative ability and consciously create our reality. Souls who fail to exercise complete control over their thought-energy projections remain cloistered within the outer, dense, training environments of the astral and physical dimensions. In order for us to enter and coexist within the instant-thought-responsive realities (the higher heavens), we must exercise complete control over our thought projections. Our current life is the basic training ground of soul.

HOW DO BELIEF SYSTEMS LIMIT OUR PERSONAL GROWTH?

Beliefs often hinder our personal evolution by misrepresenting the reality of our spiritual evolution and our capabilities as soul. The awesome reality of our multidimensional nature and our unlimited creative ability is seldom disclosed. Many belief systems produce a form of institutional dependency by distorting the truth of our spiritual path and capabilities. For example, the centuries-old belief that we require a priest to act as an intermediary for us to communicate with God is an ancient method of control and manipulation. Billions of us have been taught from childhood that we are sinful, powerless creatures who must depend on and financially support the man-made organizations that claim to represent God on Earth. The truth is a stark opposite: we are powerful, immortal, spiritual beings directly connected to God and we create our reality in every dimension with the focused energy of our thoughts.

WHAT IS THE PRIMARY OBSTACLE THAT HOLDS HUMANITY WITHIN THE PHYSICAL AND ASTRAL DIMENSIONS?

A critical issue seldom addressed is our deep-seated belief that we are physical human beings. How can we, as soul, possibly experience and reunite our spiritual essence when we continue to cling to the dense self-identity of matter? We create the blocks to our spiritual progress by the very thoughts and beliefs we hold dear.

WHAT IS THE SINGLE MOST IMPORTANT THING I CAN DO TO ENHANCE MY SPIRITUAL DEVELOPMENT?

Practice an effective method to have your own profound spiritual experience. Make this a priority.

FINAL THOUGHTS

The awesome reality of our existence is far more mind-bending than any science fiction movie or book can begin to express. We are immortal beings who have extended our conscious awareness throughout the entire breadth of our multidimensional universe. We are courageous explorers who have chosen to learn and evolve through the use of temporary vehicles of consciousness. Each life experience is orchestrated by us for our continuing education. We learn and grow at our own pace through total immersion of our consciousness in many different thought-responsive environments. This remarkable system of spiritual evolution is extremely demanding but also exceedingly effective, because all of us, without exception, will eventually graduate from the vast training grounds of form.

A life-changing decision confronts all of us: we can choose to bury our mind in beliefs or to explore and discover the truth for ourselves. Modern explorations beyond the body provide us a window into our future. We have learned that we are powerful, creative, and immortal souls, capable of molding our reality in every dimension of the universe. We have learned that death is an illusion and that our spiritual evolution continues far beyond the limits of matter and form.

We share an amazing quest: a spiritual journey through multiple thought-responsive dimensions. By developing our creative abilities and exploring our inner selves, we awaken to the profound nature of our spiritual potential. Our continuing life beyond the physical is an exciting journey of consciousness, for we create the adventures we experience, now and forever.

GLOSSARY

Assimilation: The act of adapting to and accepting the norms and limits of any established group or collective of souls.

Astral Body: The subtle energy body that most people experience after physical death. Other common terms are light body, emotional body, and energy body. This is one of many vehicles of consciousness/soul that all physical life forms possess.

Astral Dimension: The next major dimension of energy in our multiverse. A vast, many-layered energy dimension created and maintained by the collective thoughts of the local residents. Countless consensus heavens/environments exist within this dimension and most humans experience this dimension after death.

Awakening: The process of becoming consciously aware of our multidimensional/spiritual self and the illusions of form that surround us.

Awareness Now! A focus and control method; an affirmation to increase your conscious awareness within any energy body. It is used to stabilize and focus your state of consciousness during altered states, out-of-body experiences, and inner shifts of awareness.

Belief Territories: Realities created by the shared beliefs, thoughts, and collective consciousness of a group of souls. The astral and physical dimensions are dominated by belief territories. They are also commonly called consensus realities.

Block: Any form of emotion, belief, thought, or self-image that hinders our spiritual development.

Clearing: This is the process of removing the internal energy blocks of thought, ego, emotion, and fears that slow or hinder our spiritual development. It can occur during meditation, out-of-body experiences, and during the many forms of personal energy, chakra, and kundalini work.

Clear Light of the Void: A Tibetan Buddhist phrase that refers to higher spiritual dimensions existing beyond all form-based realities. The phrase, "Go to the clear light of the void" is repeated as a mantra by Buddhist monks in order to assist the consciousness of the dying individual to move inward beyond the astral dimension (bardo) and enter the higher spiritual realms.

Consensus Reality: Any reality created and maintained by the group thought of the inhabitants; these environments are structurally stable and resistant to individual thought. After death, most humans enter consensus realities that resonate with their personal development and mindset.

Construct: Any form-based reality, body, or environment created by thought. The astral realities are constructs created by the group consciousness of the inhabitants. The energy body we experience within every dimension is a construct of our consciousness and all constructs are temporary creations.

Creation Training: Extensive training classes and realities designed to instruct souls in the art of energy manipulation and the manifestation of form. The astral and physical dimensions provide extensive training in how to focus, direct, and control thought energy. The Earth is one of many training environments used for this purpose.

Dense Ones: A slang term used to describe souls who have ensnared themselves within the outer energy environments of the physical and astral dimensions. Dense ones are souls who are currently using physical or astral bodies for their spiritual evolution and mistakenly believe that they are these dense bodies.

Energy Body: The temporary vehicle of soul. A form-based body used by consciousness for self-expression within different dimensions. We possess many vibrational energy bodies, each corresponding to a dimension of the universe. The physical body is the outermost and densest of the energy bodies.

Energy Dimensions: The major vibrational energy levels or frequencies of the universe. For example, the entire physical universe is a single energy dimension.

Energy Environment: A general term to describe a specific nonphysical reality within a given dimension. Countless energy environments and realities exist within a single dimension and are created by the collective thoughts of the local inhabitants.

Energy Membrane: The convergence point separating two major vibrational dimensions of the universe. It is often perceived as a null point, a void, or a dense layer of fog between dimensions.

Evolution: The spiritual development of consciousness through the use of many different energy bodies, constructs, and learning experiences. An extensive personal-development process incorporating multiple experiences (incarnations) in different dimensional realities.

Facade: The dense, outer energy layers of the universe; the physical and astral dimensions. This has also been referred to as the epidermis of the multiverse.

Filter of Heaven: The outermost regions of our multidimensional universe (the physical and astral dimensions) that function as training environments for the education and evolution of consciousness. This filter functions to cloister the developing souls within the dense outer dimensions until they are ready to coexist within the instant-thought-responsive, higher heavens.

First Heaven: The first consensus reality experienced immediately after death. A physical-like reality where souls are met by loved ones in an environment created by the collective thoughts of the local inhabitants. Most humans experience this initial energy environment within the astral dimension.

Form Addiction: The act of accepting three-dimensional form and substance as the only valid reality. The addiction and attraction to form holds billions of souls within the outer physical and astral dimensions. Also called form locked.

Form Locked: Souls who have unknowingly imprisoned themselves within a single, three-dimensional self-image and dense energy body. This includes most souls currently inhabiting the physical and the astral dimensions.

Graduates: Souls who have spiritually evolved beyond human form and ego through repeated experiences within the physical and astral training grounds. Souls who have evolved beyond the dense training ground of matter.

Guides: Non-physical beings who assist our personal and spiritual development. Guides often specialize in specific areas of expertise and spiritual development.

Healing Centers: Nonphysical realities and facilities designed for the rehabilitation and healing of souls arriving from the physical world.

Higher Heavens: Dimensions that exist at a higher frequency than the astral. These dimensional realities are less dense than the astral and exist closer to the energy source of all creation.

Higher Self: Our core spiritual consciousness that exists beyond all form-based, ego, and thought-created identities and realities.

Higher Self Now! This is a powerful affirmation that helps to focus and direct our conscious awareness inward so we can experience our spiritual essence beyond the projections of form. Often used as a spiritual mantra for those who are close to the natural transition of consciousness we call death.

Illusions: The many diversions that slow our spiritual growth. A common term for the many flawed concepts, beliefs and conclusions we cling to.

Initiations: Spiritual tests and vibrational adjustments that are experienced before one can advance to a higher level of spiritual training. They can occur during dreams, altered states, out-of-body experiences, and physical life. Initiations are often perceived as intense challenges or dramas that are life-threatening and are repeated until a specific quality of soul is developed and internalized.

Inner Senses: Also called subtle senses, these are the nonphysical modes of perception we use when we are out of body and after death. Each energy body utilizes different modes or senses of perception.

Jumping: The act and acquired skill of moving or shifting our conscious awareness to multiple energy environments or dimensional realities.

Locking in: The ability to stabilize and focus our state of consciousness within a single reality after moving our awareness from one energy environment to another. This is one of the essential spiritual-navigation skills.

Matrix: A stable energy environment created by group thought or any consensus reality created and maintained by collective thought. The form-based realities located within the physical and astral dimensions are the direct result of thought; they are all a temporary projection of consciousness.

Moving Inward: The act of consciously moving our awareness from our outer energy body and experiencing our higher-frequency, more subtle, energy body. Out-of body and near-death experiences are classic examples of moving inward. This is one of the essential spiritual-exploration skills.

Multidimensional Universe: The entire universe, seen and unseen; a continuum of energy dimensions consisting of an unknown number of energy frequencies or levels. As we explore inward and away from matter, each nonphysical energy dimension becomes progressively less dense and increasingly more thought responsive. The physical universe is but the dense outer epidermis of the vast unseen multiverse.

Next Level Now! A focused affirmation and command to direct your awareness inward so you will experience your higher-vibrational energy body and corresponding reality. A method to move our conscious awareness inward.

Non-consensus Realities: Nonphysical environments that are easily manipulated or altered by focused thought.

Outer Worlds: The physical and astral dimensions.

Out-of-Body Experience: A general term for the separation of consciousness from the physical body. This involves the movement of our conscious awareness from the outer physical body to one of our more subtle energy bodies. Also commonly referred to as astral projection, astral travel, or soul travel.

Parallel Dimension: The unseen energy substructure of matter existing just out of phase with the physical. It is the energy level of the universe closest in vibration to the physical and the one most often experienced during out-of-body experiences. All physical objects possess a subtle energy duplicate in this dimension. This is also referred to as the real time zone, the etheric plane, or the lower astral.

Past Lives: The evolution and training of consciousness through multiple personal experiences within the physical world. A common method of spiritual development through intense experiences in form and matter.

Peeling the Onion: A meditation that enhances the process of stripping away the many layers of illusion maintained by the mind; the conscious removal of all the internal blocks, fears, and limits that hinder our spiritual progress.

Prisoners of Form: Souls who believe they are dense humanoid beings. This dense self-conception cloisters souls within the outer dimensions of the universe. Currently the majority of physical and astral inhabitants remain attached to this flawed self-conception.

Purging Thought: The act of silencing the rambling ego mind and opening to our spiritual essence.

Reality Simulations (Soul lessons): The spiritual training of soul through the use of form-based interactions and challenges. Thought projections create the dramas and experiences needed to provide the intense educational environment used to achieve the spiritual development of soul. Reality simulations are created in many dimensions (including the physical) and are repeated until the qualities of evolved soul are is internalized by each of us.

Reality Tests: Tests used to confront and confirm the thought responsiveness and stability of any energy environment. They help distinguish consensus from non-consensus realities.

Reality Training Schools: The many training environments designed for the education of soul. The Earth is one of millions of realities created for this educational process. The form-based realities of the physical and astral dimensions provide an effective environment for souls to learn through firsthand experience.

Reincarnation: Spiritual evolution through the use of multiple life experiences in the physical and astral dimensions.

Second Death: The shedding of the astral body that occurs to some individuals after their initial physical death. This is the inner shift or movement of soul (conscious awareness) from our astral body to a higher-frequency energy body. Eventually, all of us will shed our outer energy bodies as we progress inwardly into higher-vibrational dimensions.

Second Heaven: The second dimensional reality experienced by many after their orientation and assimilation into their initial nonphysical environment. For most humans, this thought-created reality is located in the higher-vibrational regions of the astral dimension.

Shifting: The movement of our conscious awareness among the various subtle nonphysical energy bodies within our selves. An out-of-body experience is the shifting of awareness from the physical body to the astral body.

Soul: Consciousness existing beyond all form-based realities— our core and eternal spiritual essence. Soul incorporates various energy vehicles for its personal evolution and expression, including the mind, emotions, and all manifestations of form, both physical and nonphysical.

Soul Group: A group of souls who evolve together through the use of shared social interactions, challenges, and dramas. They often incarnate as family units and social groups as they share and repeat karmic lessons.

Source: A common term for God, creator, or ultimate spiritual home.

Third Heaven: A highly thought-responsive dimension inhabited by souls focused on their creative and spiritual development.

Thought Forms: Subtle nonphysical (astral) forms of energy that are shaped and molded by the creative power of thought. These energy forms may appear as any size or density.

Tunnel or Membrane Opening: An opening or portal within an energy membrane separating different vibrational dimensions. It is sometimes perceived to be an energetic opening, door, or tunnel entrance during near-death and out-of-body experiences.

Vibrational State: An energy event reported immediately before and after an out-of-body experience; this may involve one or all of the following: internal vibrations, energy sensations, sounds, voices, music, floating, and temporary paralysis. Please refer to *Adventures Beyond the Body* for additional details.

Virtual-Reality Training Environments: Three dimensional realities that provide countless opportunities for the evolution of soul through intense personal experiences. Earth is but one of these reality training environments. They are also called energy simulations and consensus realities. Complete immersion within these training environments is one of the primary methods used for the spiritual evolution of consciousness.

The
Energy Mechanics
of Creation
(The Training Ground of the Soul)

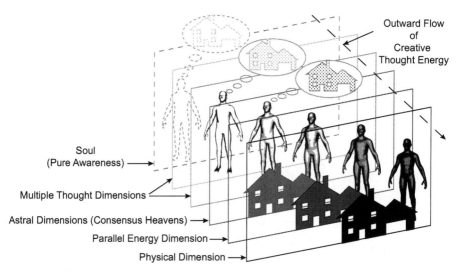

All of creation begins as thought and expands outward in density.
Focused thoughts create the energy molds (thought forms) within
the nonphysical dimensions and act as the sub structure for matter.

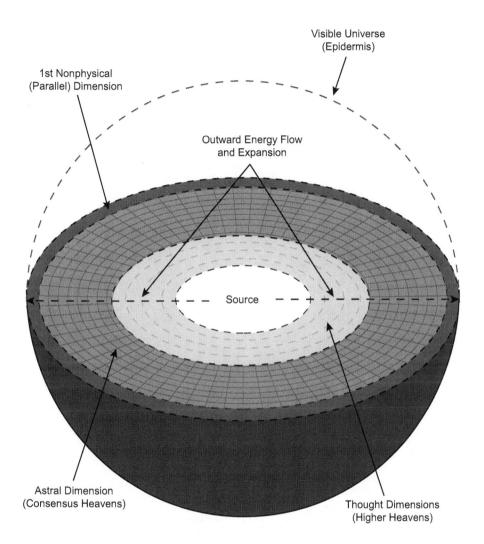

The Expanding Multidimensional Universe

The expansion of the physical universe is the direct result of the thought energy expansion occurring within the inner dimensions.

The Filter of Heaven

(The Evolution of Soul Through Form)

Individual learning experiences into the physical universe
and back to the astral dimension (multiple journeys)

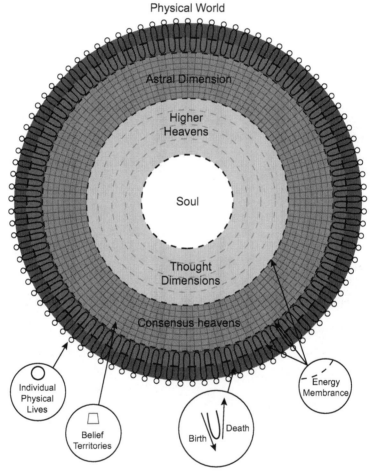

The evolution of soul through extensive experiences within form-based realities.
Humans remain cloistered within the dense outer dimensions until they develop
the qualities of an evolved soul. Millions of consensus realities exist created
by the collective thoughts of the inhabitants.

The Multidimensional Nature of all Physical Life

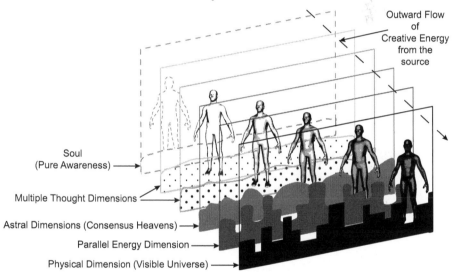

Outward Flow of Creative Energy from the source

Soul (Pure Awareness)

Multiple Thought Dimensions

Astral Dimensions (Consensus Heavens)

Parallel Energy Dimension

Physical Dimension (Visible Universe)

Each inner dimension is progressively less dense and more thought responsive

ACKNOWLEDGEMENTS

I would like to thank all of my book and audio publishers for their continuing support and commitment to my work. In addition, I appreciate the many radio show hosts and convention organizers that have helped to shed light on the importance of out-of-body experiences as a profound exploration of our spiritual nature.

I would also like to express my gratitude for all the important work that is done at the Monroe Institute. The entire staff is dedicated to providing the best possible experience for all the workshop participants. Much appreciation goes out to Carol de la Herran who, as President, works tirelessly pulling it all together, enabling the Monroe Institute to continue to provide a great opportunity for personal exploration and spiritual growth. I encourage everyone to check out their website www.monroeinstitute.com. There are many excellent programs for the exploration of consciousness.

Ken Elliott, thanks for being my web master. You are an extraordinary fine artist and more important, my friend.

I would like to thank Patty Avalon who helps to keep my Monroe Institute out-of-body exploration workshops running smoothly and fun.

Thanks go to Eric Buhlman for the redesign and maintenance of my website, www.astralinfo.org.

Many thanks to Claudia Carlton Lambright, for the many hours you spend keeping the Yahoo OBE Newsletter forum lively and relevant. It wouldn't be the same without your great skills as an excellent moderator.

I would like to thank April Hannah and Mike Habernig for their fine work in creating, *The Path* documentaries. www.thepathseries.com.

Thanks to Marianne Pestana who has helped to show me how the media can be an asset.

I wish to express my sincere gratitude to Greg Brooks for the diagrams and illustrations. I deeply regret the passing of Greg before he could see his work published.

My sincere thanks go to the past presidents of the Monroe Institute for their support, F. Holmes "Skip" Atwater and Paul Rademacher.

Karen Doll at (www.karen659.blogspot.com) is one of the most prolific and inspiring writers I have seen on the topic of out of body exploration. Her experiences and advice have helped many to examine out-of-body travel as a serious method of inner exploration and spiritual evolution.

My gratitude goes out to Dr. Art Roffey and Gail Danto for their years of support and friendship. I recommend Dr. Roffey's work in self-discovery and personal growth. Contact information can be found at www.innervisionpc.org.

Thanks to Richard and Ann Hutchinson in Arizona for continuing to provide a venue for out-of-body exploration in the southwest. I look forward to our next workshop in Sedona.

I would also like to thank Tom Carey at www.mach1audio.com for his continuing support.

Many thanks to all my great friends and workshop organizers around the world: Franck Labat in France; Fabio Moschetta in Venice, Italy; Sandro Sestili in Rome, Italy; Pietro Ugazzi in Lugano, Switzerland; Marina Ciaffonini of Harmonia Mundi in Rome; and Mr. Emai, president of Natural Spirit Company in Japan. I would also like thank my Italian interpreter, Maja Bodo, for her excellent work. Because of all your efforts, we have helped to expand the subject of out-of-body exploration as an international topic of study and an effective spiritual practice.

RESOURCES

Journeys Out of the Body by Robert A. Monroe
Far Journeys by Robert A. Monroe
The Holographic Universe by Michael Talbot
The Unanswered Question by Kurt Leland
Multi-Dimensional Man by Jurgen Ziewe
My Big TOE by Thomas Campbell
Handbook to the Afterlife by Pamela Rae Heath and Jon Klimo
The Power of Now by Eckhart Tolle
Exploring the World of Lucid Dreaming by Stephen La Berge
Seth Speaks by Jane Roberts
Out-of-Body Experiences by Robert Peterson
Life after Life by Raymond Moody
Power vs. Force by David Hawkings
Journey of Souls by Michael Newton
Spiritual Growth: Being your Higher Self by Sanaya Roman
Many Lives, Many Masters by Brian Weiss
The Omega Project by Kenneth Ring
The Seat of the Soul by Gary Zukav
Illusions by Richard Bach

The Tibetan Book of the Dead
Adventures beyond the Body by William Buhlman
The Secret of the Soul by William Buhlman

Film
The Path: Beyond the Physical by Mike Habernig and April Hannah

Biography of William Buhlman

William Buhlman is one of the world's leading experts on the subject of out-of-body experiences. With over forty years of extensive personal out-of-body exploration, he brings a unique and thought provoking insight into this subject. His first book, *Adventures beyond the Body* chronicles his own personal journey of self-discovery through out-of-body travel, and further provides the reader with the preparation and techniques that can be used for their own adventure.

The provocative results of Buhlman's international out-of-body experience survey that includes over 16,000 participants from forty-two countries are presented in his book, *The Secret of the Soul*. This cutting edge material explores the unique opportunities for personal growth and profound spiritual awakenings that have been reported during out-of-body experiences.

Over the past two decades William has developed an effective system to experience safe, self-initiated out-of-body adventures. His in-depth six-day workshop entitled, *Out-of-Body Exploration Intensive* is held at the renowned Monroe Institute in Virginia. As a certified hypnotherapist, William incorporates various methods, including hypnosis, visualization and meditation techniques in his workshops to explore the profound nature of out-of-body experiences and the benefits of accelerated personal development. In addition, he has developed an extensive series of audio programs designed to expand awareness and assist in the exploration of consciousness.

William has been the featured speaker at conferences worldwide, as well as, the workshop leader in Venice, Rome, Lyon, London, Tokyo, and Caracas, to name a few. His objective is to teach people how to have profound spiritual adventure. William has also appeared on television's "Sightings" and in "The Path" documentaries, along with over one hundred radio shows.

William's books are currently available in twelve languages. The author lives in Delaware, USA. For more information visit the author's web site, www.astralinfo.org.

Made in the USA
Middletown, DE
08 April 2022